T0064378

Uncovering The General Economic Logic Of Price Systems

John P. Barrados, Ph.D. (Columbia)

Studies In Economic Theory

Order this book online at www.trafford.com
or email orders@trafford.com

Most Trafford titles are also available at major online book retailers.

Print information available on the last page.

ISBN: 978-1-4669-9485-0 (sc)
ISBN: 978-1-4669-9484-3 (e)

Library of Congress Control Number: 2013909273

Trafford rev. 05/27/2021

 www.trafford.com

North America & international
toll-free: 844-688-6899 (USA & Canada)
fax: 812 355 4082

Table Of Contents

Preface

The price theory literature is characterized by microeconomic and macroeconomic systems. Microeconomic systems deal with the detailed behaviour of the individual and the firm. While macroeconomic systems deal with broad aggregates that usually do not stem in a precise way from the behavior of the individual and the firm. This approach, however, leads to systems that are restricted in generality.

This is reflected, for example, in orthodox microeconomic and macroeconomic systems being dichotomized which subjects the systems to additional problems. These various problems will be covered in detail later in the book.

Orthodox microeconomic and macroeconomic systems are dichotomized because neither system reflects what we shall refer to as the *general economic logic* that should underlie all price systems. This is a logic that applies to all price systems irrespective of the different forms of behavior of individual systems.

We suggest in this book that prior to writing specific price systems, we should first isolate this general economic logic of price systems. We should then write particular systems that reflect different forms of behavior, to conform to this general economic logic.

This is the approach to price systems set out in this book, an approach that will rid orthodox price systems of the dichotomy between orthodox microeconomic and macroeconomic systems and of basic problems that arise on account of this dichotomy.

However, to bring the general economic logic to which we referred into orthodox price systems requires resolving an inconsistency in the orthodox microecoonomic systems. Let us describe this inconsistency.

Price systems are all necessarily *subject* to limitation in resources. Hence the systems should reflect *consistency* with limitation in resources.

We define consistency with limited resources to be reflected in the quantities of commodities demanded and supplied in price systems each summing to the systems' limited resources to hence exhaust these resources.

Consistency with limitation in resources applies to all price systems. Hence we may look on consistency with limited resources as reflecting the *general logic* of the systems.

That is, a logic that characterizes all price systems irrespective of the differing forms of behavior of individual systems.

We shall take the orthodox classical system which we shall refer to as Model A, as representative of orthodox microeconomic price systems.

Next, we shall form a revised classical system, to be referred to as Model B, which we shall take as representative of our new microeconomic systems. Let us first consider the orthodox classical system, Model A, which we shall set out in detail in Chapter 3.

Consistency of a system with limited resources should be ensured by the behavior of individuals and firms in the system. However, we shall find that Model A lacks an aspect to behavior that should ensure consistency of the system with limitation in resources.

This as we shall establish, results in consistency of Model A with limited resources being ensured in a non-behavioral manner. This brings inconsistency into the system since consistency of a system with limited resources should be ensured by the behavior in the system.

Model A does reflect the *general logic* of price systems in reflecting consistency with limitation in resources. However, Model A does not reflect the *general economic logic* of price systems.

This is because consistency of the system with limitation in resources is not ensured by the behavior in the system but is ensured in a non-behavioral manner. Let us now consider Model B, our revised form of Model A.

We shall incorporate into Model B through the system's demand and supply functions, an aspect to behavior that ensures consistency of the system with limitation in resources. Hence through Model B, we shall resolve the inconsistency of Model A.

Consequently, Model B will reflect the *general economic logic* of price systems since unlike Model A, consistency with limitation in resources will be ensured in Model B by the behavior in the system.

There are various consequences of our resolving through Model B, the inconsistency we uncover in orthodox microeconomic price systems, systems we represent by Model A, the orthodox classical system.

Keynes has held that the orthodox classical system, Model A, is restricted to long-run states by Say's Law. However, we shall find that this is due to the inconsistency we have uncovered in the system.

Hence in ridding Model B of this inconsistency, we shall find that the latter system is not restricted by Say's Law to long-run states.

Moreover, as will be discussed in Chapter 7, Model B will be rid of the price level indeterminacy and invalid real-monetary dichotomy that characterize the neoclassical form of Model A, problems brought out by Patinkin.

Next, our analysis as will be discussed in Chapter 10, will allow us to arrive at an improved criterion for ensuring consistency of price systems. There is yet a further contribution of the book. The orthodox classical system which we represent by Model A, predates Keynesian analysis.

However, when Keynes set out his macroeconomic system, this latter system remained dichotomized from the orthodox classical microeconomic system. This microeconomic-macroeconomic dichotomy will be resolved in the book along the following lines.

In ridding the orthodox classical system Model A of inconsistency, we arrive at our revised classical system, Model B. However, this latter system is incomplete in lacking an overall output or income variable.

This is because the system's functions determine only relative quantities of commodities demanded (supplied). However, in Chapter 11, we shall set out a very general system, Model C, that completes Model B.

This is by our incorporating into Model B a Keynesian overall output or income variable which reflects the system's limited flow of resources. This leads to Model C, this latter system integrating microeconomic and macroeconomic analysis in the following way.

The microeconomics of Model C in stemming from Model B, ensures consistency of Model C with limitation in resources. While these resources stem from the Keynesian system.

Hence as will be discussed in detail in Chapter 11, microeconomic and macroeconomic analysis in Model C are complementary and are thereby integrated in the system.

In sum, through Model C we integrate our revised classical system, namely, the microeconomic Model B, with the Keynesian macroeconomic system.

Moreover, we shall discuss in Chapter 11 how such an integration is impossible when Model A, rather than Model B, is taken as the orthodox classical system.

My introduction to economic analysis was at McGill University where I benefitted considerably from courses in economic theory given by Professors David McCord Wright and Earl F. Beach.

I am also indebted to Professors William S. Vickrey and Phillip David Cagan of Columbia University for their help with a dissertation on price theory which I wrote at Columbia.

An outcome of my work in price theory has been a number of published papers as well as the present book. Among my published papers is an early one of relevance to this book. See *"A Solution to the Problem of the Inconsistency of the Classical Exchange Model," Kyklos, 1972.*

Dr. John P. Barrados,
Barrados Consultants,
22 Whippoorwill Drive,
Ottawa, ON K1J 7J2,
Canada.
April, 2021.

Chapter 1

An Inconsistency In Orthodox Microeconomic Price Systems

1.1 Introduction

We shall review in this chapter, the inconsistency we described that characterizes orthodox microeconomic price systems. These are systems we represent by Model A, the orthodox classical system. As well, we shall review how we shall resolve this inconsistency through Model B, our revised classical system.

Model A, the orthodox classical system, was developed in neoclassical analysis but is also widely taken as a formal version of the classical system.

Hence while we may refer to Model A as classical or neoclassical, we shall find it convenient to take it as a classical system.[1] Nonetheless, there is a digression Chapter 7 when Model A is taken as a neoclassical system. This is in order to deal with Patinkin's criticisms of the latter system

We shall also develop a revised form of Model A which we shall refer to as Model B. That is, the latter system is our revised classical system. Model B puts Model A, the orthodox classical system, into a more general form.

This is accomplished by our bringing into Model B through the system's functions, an aspect to the behavior of individuals and firms that is missing from Model A. This is an aspect to behavior that ensures consistency of Model B with limitation in resources.

This aspect to behavior is of such a general character that it allows us to preserve in Model B, the basic character of Model A

---

[1] This system appears in many places in the literature being called at times a classical system and at other times a neoclassical system. See, for example, W.B.Hickman, "The Determinacy of Absolute Prices in Classical Economic Theory," *Econometrica*, 1950, where it is called a classical system. However, see Don Patinkin *Money, Interest, And Prices* (2nd. ed., Harper and Row, New York, 1965), esp. Ch. VIII, where it is called a neoclassical system.

as a long-run, microeconomic system. However, Model B will have a more general character than Model A.

This is because Model B will be characterized by an aspect to behavior that ensures consistency of the system with limitation in resources, an aspect to behavior that is missing from Model A. This means that Model B will reflect the *general economic logic* that should underlie all price systems.

Model A, in contrast, lacks an aspect to behavior that ensures consistency of the system with limited resources. Hence while Model A reflects the *general logic* of price systems in reflecting consistency with limited resources, the system does not reflect the *general economic logic* of price systems.

This is because consistency of Model A with limited resources is not ensured by the behavior in the system which accounts for the inconsistency we uncover in the system. This chapter also covers in a preliminary way a basic consequence of our resolving Model A's inconsistency through Model B.

This is reflected in Model B being rid of what we shall find is a misused Say's Law that characterizes Model A and which restricts the latter system to long-run states.

Yet Model B will reflect Say's Law but a correctly-used form of the Law. This as we shall establish in Chapter 6 is a true identity that is simply a descriptive device that hence cannot possibly restrict the system to long-run states.

There will be a great deal of focus in the book on how consistency of price systems is ensured. Hence we shall draw on what we shall refer to as the "counting rule" that is used to ensure consistency of price systems.

This rule is that for a system to be consistent, the number of independent equations and unknown variables in a system must be equal. We shall find that this rule is met in Model B on account of the new aspect to behavior that we shall incorporate into the system.

However, since this aspect to behavior is missing from Model A, this system meets this rule in a non-behavioral manner. This we shall find is through Say's Law being imposed on the system to eliminate a surplus equation. However, the Law which we shall consider in detail later in the book, restricts Model A to long-run states.

Model B, in contrast, will not be restricted in this way since we do not need to impose the Law on the system to ensure that it meets the counting rule. This is because Model B will meet this rule on account of the behavior in the system.

Consequently, Model B will be rid of the misused Say's Law that is imposed on Model A to eliminate a surplus equation but which restricts the system to long-run states.

Yet as we noted, Model B will be characterized by the Law but a true identity form of the Law that hence cannot possibly restrict the system to long-run states.

1.2 Review Of The Inconsistency In Orthodox Microeconomic Systems

Price systems are necessarily *subject* to limitation in resources. Hence the systems should reflect *consistency* with limitation in resources. We defined consistency with limited resources to be reflected in the quantities of commodities demanded and supplied in price systems each summing to the systems' limited or given resources to hence exhaust these resources.

Moreover, since consistency of price systems applies to all systems, we take such consistency to reflect the *general logic* of the systems.

We also discussed how we shall take the orthodox classical system, Model A, as representative of orthodox microeconomic price systems. As well, we shall set out a revised classical system, to be referred to as Model B, which we shall take as representative of our new microeconomic systems.

Let us consider Model A, the orthodox classical system, which we shall set out in detail in Chapter 3. We shall find that the system lacks an aspect to behavior that should ensure consistency of the system with limitation in resources. Consistency of the system with limited resources is then ensured in a non-behavioral manner.

This brings inconsistency into the system since consistency of the system with limited resources should be ensured by the behavior in the system. Model A does reflect the *general logic* of price systems in reflecting consistency with limitation in resources.

However, Model A does not reflect the *general economic logic* of price systems. This is because consistency of the system with limitation in resources is not ensured by the behavior in the system. Let us now consider Model B which is our revised form of Model A.

We shall incorporate into Model B through the system's functions, an aspect to behavior that ensures consistency of the system with limitation in resources. This is an aspect to behavior that is missing from Model A.

Hence through Model B we shall resolve the inconsistency of Model A. This will account for Model B being be rid of a misused Say's Law that characterizes Model A and which restricts the latter system to long-run states.

Moreover, as will be discussed in Chapter 7, Model B will also be rid of the price level indeterminacy and invalid real-monetary dichotomy that Patinkin showed characterize the neoclassical form of Model A.

As well, we shall come upon an improved criterion for consistency of price systems, see Chapter 10. Finally, our analysis as will be discussed in Chapter 11, allows us to form systems in which microeconomic and macroeconomic analysis are integrated.

1.3 The Orthodox And The New Approach To Price Systems

By the orthodox approach to price systems, we mean the approach that is the basis of orthodox microeconomic price systems, systems we represent by Model A, the orthodox classical system.

This approach is based on individuals and firms demanding and supplying goods, subject to a budget constraint, to maximize their utility and profit. This behavior, in turn, leads to demand and supply functions that apply to each individual and firm.

These demand and supply functions of individuals and firms are then aggregated to form market demand and supply functions on which market price systems are based. This, of course, is the standard approach to orthodox microeconomic price systems, systems we represent by Model A.

Let us sketch how this approach will be revised in this book though our new systems which we represent by Model B, our revised classical system.

We shall show that an aspect to behavior that should ensure consistency of price systems with limited resources is missing from orthodox microeconomic price systems.

This results in the orthodox or neoclassical-type demand and supply functions, while reflecting the behavior of particular systems, suppressing the *general economic logic* that should underlie all price systems. This is because the orthodox-type functions do not reflect behavior that is consistent with limitation in resources.

However, we shall bring the aspect to behavior that is missing from orthodox price systems into our new systems. This will be accomplished through a new type of demand and supply functions that will be set out in Chapters 5 and 6.

These new functions which will form the basis for Model B will not only reflect the behavior of this particular system. As well, the functions will capture the *general economic logic* that should underlie all price systems. This is because these new functions will reflect behavior that is consistent with limitation in resources.

On the other hand, the orthodox or neoclassical-type demand and supply functions such as characterize Model A, do not reflect the general economic logic that characterizes our new systems. This is because Model A's functions do not reflect behavior that is consistent with limitation in resources.

This restricts the generality of Model A, the orthodox classical system, compared to Model B, our revised classical system. This will be reflected in various ways, for example in Model A being restricted to long-run states by a misused Say's Law whereas Model B will not be restricted in this way.

1.4 Ensuring Consistency Of Price Systems

Let us review the orthodox rules for consistency of price systems. These rules are centered on the need to ensure equality between the number of independent equations and the number of unknowns of the system. That is, to ensure that the "counting rule" referred to in Section 1.1 is met.

There are as economists have pointed out various qualifications to this counting rule. [2] Economists, however, generally take equality between the number of independent equations and unknowns of a system to mean that it is reasonable to assume that the system is consistent.

This is in the sense that one set of variables can simultaneously satisfy every equation of the system. Moreover, it is also usually assumed that only one such set of variables exists.

However, while all price systems must meet the counting rule in order to be consistent, we shall find that this rule occupies quite a different place in Model B, our revised classical system, compared to Model A, the orthodox classical system.

---

[2] See, for example, William S. Vickrey, *Microstatics* (New York, 1964), see pages 121-22.

This is because while it is a rule or condition that must be met in all systems, meeting this condition in Model B will be a consequence of the system's behavior or economic rationale. Hence it is not a rule to be imposed on Model B since it is ensured by the behavior or economic rationale of the system.

In contrast, we shall find that Model A does not meet the counting rule on account of the system's behavior or economic rationale. Instead, the counting rule is imposed on Model A by Say's Law being used to eliminate a surplus equation from the system. But the Law restricts the system to long-run states.

However, a system should meet the counting rule on account of the behavior of the system. This will be the case with Model B which will result in the system being rid of a misused Say's Law that is imposed on Model A to eliminate a surplus equation but which restricts the system long-run states.

Nonetheless, as will be established in Chapter 6.4, Model B will yet be characterized by the Law but a true identity form of the Law that hence cannot possibly restrict the system to long-run states.

1.5 Summary

We described in the preface and in this chapter an inconsistency that we have uncovered in orthodox microeconomic price systems, systems we represent by Model A, the orthodox classical system.

This system is inconsistent in an economic sense because it lacks an aspect to the behavior of individuals and firms. This is an aspect to behavior that should ensure consistency of the system with limitation in resources.

That is, the aspect to behavior that should ensure that the quantities of commodities demanded (supplied) each sum to the system's limited resources to hence exhaust these resources.

Next, since Model A lacks this aspect to behavior, the system is made consistent with limited resources in a non-behavioral manner. This as we shall establish in Chapter 5 is on account of Say's Law.

We shall, however, resolve Model A's inconsistency through Model B. This is because consistency of the latter system with limited resources will be ensured by the behavior of individuals and firms rather than by the non-behavioral Say's Law as is the case with Model A.

Consequently, we shall rid Model B of Say's Law that ensures consistency of Model A with limitation in resources but which restricts the latter system to long-run states.

However, as will also be established in Chapter 6.4, Model B will yet be characterized by the Law but a true identity form of the Law that hence cannot possibly restrict the system to long-run states.

Chapter 2

Remarks On The Inconsistency In Orthodox Microeconomic Price Systems

2.1 Introduction

We described in the preface and the previous chapter the inconsistency that we have uncovered in orthodox microeconomic price systems, systems we represent by Model A, the orthodox classical system.

This inconsistency, to review, arises because Model A lacks an aspect to behavior that should ensure consistency of the system with limited resources.

Hence as we also discussed, Model A, while reflecting the *general logic* of price systems in reflecting consistency with limited resources, does not reflect the *general economic logic* that should underlie all price systems.

This is because consistency of Model A with limited resources is not ensured by the behavior in the system but is ensured in a non-behavioral manner.

Model A's inconsistency, however, will be resolved through Model B since consistency of the latter system with limitation in resources will be ensured by the behavior in the system. This means, to review, that Model B, unlike Model A, will reflect the *general economic logic* that should underlie all price systems.

We shall also discuss in more detail how our analysis provides a solution to the problem of Say's Law restricting the orthodox classical system to long-run states. Finally, we shall discuss why the inconsistency of Model A remained hidden.

2.2 Ensuring Consistency Of Price Systems

Model A is inconsistent in an economic sense because the system's demand and supply functions do not ensure consistency of the system with limitation in resources. That is, the system's functions do not ensure that the quantities of commodities demanded (supplied) each sum to the system's given or limited resources to hence exhaust these resources.

This we shall find results in the system being characterized by a surplus equation over the number of unknowns. Economists then impose Say's Law on the system to eliminate this surplus to ensure that the system meets the counting rule.

Moreover, as we shall discuss in Chapter 5, the Law also ensures that Model A is consistent with limitation in resources. Hence the non-behavioral Say's Law is given preference over the behavior in the system in ensuring that Model A is consistent with limitation in resources.

In contrast, Model B's demand and supply functions will reflect behavior that ensures consistency of the system with limitation in resources.

Consequently, we shall remove from Model B the invalid role that Say's Law plays in Model A of ensuring consistency of the latter system with limitation in resources. Hence Model B will be rid of Say's Law that ensures consistency of Model A with limited resources.

In sum, we shall ensure that consistency of Model B with limitation in resources is ensured by the behavior in the system. Hence through Model B we shall resolve the inconsistency we have uncovered in Model A.

This, to review, is because Model A's inconsistency arises because the system is made consistent with limitation in resources by the non-behavioral Say's Law rather than by the behavior in the system.

2.3 The Budget Constraints Of The Orthodox And Revised Classical Systems

Much of the focus of the book will be on how consistency of price systems with limitation in resources is to be ensured. Next, we defined consistency with limited resources of a system as being reflected in the quantities of commodities demanded (supplied) each summing to the system's limited resources to hence exhaust these resources.

This means that in dealing with the issue of consistency of price systems with limited resources, we are dealing with the systems' budget constraints. This is because budget constraints arise on account of limitation in resources.

Next, we shall establish in Chapter 5, that consistency with limited resources is ensured in Model A by Say's Law. This implies that Say's Law in Model A is a budget constraint. Moreover, since the Law is imposed on Model A from the outside, this means that the Law in the system is an externally-imposed budget constraint.

However, the Law and hence the system's external budget constraint restricts the system to long-run states. This means that the Law in Model A is not a true identity since were it a true identity it could not possibly restrict the system to long-run states. Let us now consider Model B.

We shall find as will be discussed in Chapter 6, that consistency with limited resources is ensured in Model B by the behavior in the system. Moreover, as is the case with Model A, consistency with limited resources in Model B implies that the system is subject to a budget constraint.

Hence since consistency with limited resources of Model B stems from the behavior in the system, the system's budget constraint also stems from the behavior in the system. This we shall find, accounts for Model B's budget constraint being determined *within* the system.

Consequently, this budget constraint in being internal to the system, cannot possibly restrict the system to long-run states. This as we shall also find in Chapter 6, accounts for this internal budget constraint being a true identity form of Say's Law.

In sum, we shall resolve the issue of Model A being restricted by the Law to long-run states by dealing with the Law in terms of budget constraints.

Then we shall establish that Say's Law in Model A is an externally-imposed budget constraint that restricts the system to long-run states hence it is not a true identity.

However, Model A's external budget constraint will be transformed into an internal budget constraint in Model B. This budget constraint, in being internal to Model B, cannot possibly restrict the system to long-run states.

This as we shall establish in Chapter 6 gives Model B's internal budget constraint the property of being a true identity form of Say's Law that hence cannot possibly restrict the system to long-run states.

2.4 Further Remarks On The Inconsistency In Orthodox Price Systems

We find it convenient to deal with orthodox microeconomic price systems in this book by focusing on the orthodox classical system, Model A. However, the inconsistency we have uncovered in Model A characterizes all price systems that are based on the same general approach as Model A. This is readily established.

Orthodox price systems like Model A are characterized by external budget constraints this being Say's Law in the case of Model A. These external budget constraints restrict the systems to particular states just as Say's Law, which is Model A's external budget constraint, restricts this system to long-run states.

Moreover, these external budget constraints ensure consistency of the systems with limited resources. Hence the inconsistency of Model A that we described characterizes all orthodox microeconomic systems.

This is because consistency of the systems with limited resources should be ensured by the behavior in the systems rather than by non-behavioral budget constraints.

However, following our analysis of Model B in the previous section, we shall resolve this inconsistency by ensuring that consistency with limited resources in Model B is ensured by the behavior in the systems.

Next, again following our analysis of Model B in the previous section, this will ensure that the budget constraints of our new systems are determined *within* the systems. Hence these internal budget constraints cannot possibly restrict our new systems to any particular states.

This will account for these budget constraints being transformed into true identities that hence cannot possibly restrict the systems to any particular states.

This in the case of Model B, as will be discussed in Chapter 6.4, will be reflected in the system's internal budget constraint being a true identity form of Say's Law that hence cannot possibly restrict the system to long-run states.

In sum, again following our analysis in the previous section, we shall in resolving the inconsistency we uncover in orthodox price systems, simultaneously resolve in the following way, the issue of orthodox price systems being restricted to particular states by external budget constraints.

This is by our establishing that in resolving the inconsistency we uncovered in the systems, these external budget

11

constraints will be transformed in our new systems into internal budget constraints.

These constraints, in being internal to the systems, cannot possibly restrict the systems to any particular states. This will give these internal budget constraints the property of being true identities that hence cannot possibly restrict the systems to any particular states.

2.5 Say's Law And The Classical And Keynesian Systems Law

Keynes held that Model A is restricted by Say's Law to long-run states. However, we shall establish that while Model A is indeed restricted to long-run states by Say's Law as Keynes held, this is because the system is characterized by a misused form of the Law; and it is this misused Say's Law that restricts Model A to long-run states.

Economists in setting out Model A write Say's Law as an identity. However, as discussed earlier, we shall establish that the Law ensures consistency of the system with limited resources.

This explains why we concluded that there is a misused Say's Law in Model A; since a correctly used Say's Law, in being a true identity, should not be given the substantive role of ensuring consistency of the system with limited resources.

In sum, we recognize in this book that Model A is characterized by a misused Say's Law which accounts for the system being restricted to long-run states. Hence the solution to this is to bring a correct form of the Law into Model A. This is the approach we follow in this book through Model B.

Keynes, instead, wholly removed Model A's misused Say's Law from his system. This was through Keynes forming aggregate demand and supply functions that allow the aggregate demand and supply of commodities in his system to diverge.

These aggregative functions, however, suppress the microeconomics of the parts of the Keynesian system that are based on such functions.

In contrast, we shall rid Model B of Model A's misused Say's Law by our transforming this misused Say's Law from being an externally-imposed budget constraint in the case of Model A into an internal budget constraint in Model B.

This internal budget constraint of Model B we shall find in Chapter 6 is a true identity form of Say's Law that hence cannot possibly restrict the system to long-run states.

Moreover, individual quantities of commodities demanded (supplied) emerge from this budget constraint which reflects how Model B is wholly microeconomic in character.

In sum, Model B like the Keynesian system, is not restricted to long-run states by Model A's misused Say's Law. However, Model B unlike the Keynesian system, is wholly microeconomic in character.

2.6 Contrasting How Consistency Of Model A And Model B Is Ensured

We have discussed how consistency is imposed on Model A through the imposing of the counting rule on the system. This is accomplished through Say's Law being used to eliminate a surplus equation from the system. However, Say's Law restricts Model A to long-run states.

We need, of course, to ensure that price systems meet the counting rule. However, we need to apply this rule to Model A in a manner that does not result in the system being restricted to long-run states. This will be accomplished in the following way.

We shall establish that Say's Law, in being imposed on Model A to eliminate a surplus equation, simultaneously ensures that the system is consistent with limitation in resources.

This brings inconsistency into the system since consistency of Model A with limitation in resources should be ensured by the behavior in the system.

This means that if we could find a behavioral means to ensure consistency of Model A with limited resources, we would rid the system of the role of Say's Law of ensuring that the system is consistent with limitation in resources. Hence we would avoid Model A's inconsistency.

Nonetheless, this behavioral approach to ensuring consistency of Model A with limitation in resources would yet have to ensure that the number of independent equations and unknowns are equal as called for by the counting rule.

We shall establish that the new aspect to behavior that we shall bring into Model B ensures consistency of the system with limitation resources.

Moreover, as will be discussed in Chapter 6.3, this new aspect to behavior also ensures equality between of the number of independent equations and unknowns in the system. That is, Model B will automatically meet the counting rule.

Consequently, we do not have to *impose* the counting rule on Model B through Say's Law as has to be done in the case of Model A. This is because the behavior in Model B ensures that the system meets the counting rule.

This will account for Model B being rid of Say's Law that is imposed on Model A to eliminate a surplus equation but which restricts the system to long-run states. Yet Model B will be characterized by the Law, but a true identity form of the Law that cannot possibly restrict the system to long-run states.

2.7 Further Remarks On Model A And Say's Law

Say's Law is a non-behavioral element that is imposed on Model A to eliminate a surplus equation from the system. This as we have discussed, accounts for the system being characterized by a misused form of the Law that restricts the system to long-run states.

However, we cannot simply remove the Law from the system; since we would return to Model A in its initial state where it is characterized by a surplus equation over the number of unknowns.

We have to rid Model A of its misused Say's Law by finding a behavioral substitute for this misused Law. Let us review how this will be accomplished.

Say's Law not only rids Model A of a surplus equation but as we shall establish in detail in Chapter 5.2, the Law also ensures consistency of the system with limited resources.

This is a reflection of the inconsistency in the system since consistency of the system with limited resources should be ensured by the behavior in the system.

However, we shall resolve Model A's inconsistency through Model B by bringing into the latter system an aspect to behavior that ensures consistency of the system with limited resources.

This means that Say's Law in Model B is rid of the invalid role imputed to the Law in Model A of ensuring consistency of the latter system with limitation in resources.

This accounts for Model B being rid of Model A's misused Say's Law that ensures consistency of the system with limited resources but which restricts the system to long-run states.

This will be confirmed by our establishing in Chapter 6.4 that Model B is characterized by a correctly-used Say's Law. This we shall find is a true identity that hence cannot possibly restrict the system to long-run states.

2.8 Why The Inconsistency Of Model A Was Hidden

Model A, to review, is subject to an economic inconsistency. This is because the system's demand and supply functions, and hence the behavior or economic rationale of the system, does not ensure that the system is consistent with limitation in resources.

That is, Model A's functions do not ensure that the quantities of commodities demanded (supplied) each sum to the system's limited resources to hence exhaust these resources.

This results in Model A being characterized by a surplus equation over the number of unknowns. Economists then usually ensure consistency of Model A by imposing Say's Law on the system to eliminate the system's surplus equation.

This, as we shall establish in Chapter 5.2, simultaneously ensures that the system is consistent with limitation in resources. Consequently, Say's Law is misused in Model A.

This is because the system's initial inconsistency, as reflected in the system being characterized by a surplus equation, is the result of an economic inconsistency, the latter being a consequence of the system lacking an aspect to behavior that should ensure consistency of the system with limited resources.

As a result, making Model A consistent by imposing Say's Law on the system to eliminate a surplus equation implies using the non-behavioral Law to resolve an economic inconsistency in the system, which is impossible.

Consequently, Model A remains inconsistent in an economic sense; since while the system reflects consistency with limited resources, this is not ensured by the behavior in the system. Model A's economic inconsistency, however, remained hidden.

This is because this inconsistency results in the system being characterized by a surplus equation over the number of unknowns. Economists then ensure that Model A is consistent by using Say's Law to eliminate the system's surplus equation leading them to conclude that the system is consistent.

This shifted into the background the whole issue of how consistency of Model A with limited resources should be ensured by the behavior in the system.

This is because Model A *seems* to be consistent in that the number of independent equations and the number of unknowns in the system are equal.

However, the system was deemed to be consistent on the basis of meeting the counting rule rather than on the basis of being consistent in an economic sense. This is because while Model A meets the counting rule, hidden within the system is the economic inconsistency we have uncovered.

This, to review, is reflected in consistency of Model A with limitation in resources being ensured by Say's Law rather than being ensured by the behavior in the system. Let us sketch how this will be resolved.

We shall revise Model A through Model B, by ensuring that consistency of the latter system with limitation in resources is ensured by the behavior in the system. This means that Model B will be rid of Model A's inconsistency. This as will be discussed in Chapter 6.3 will also ensure that Model B automatically meets the counting rule.

Hence consistency of Model B in the sense of the system meeting the counting rule will be a *result* of the system's economic consistency. That is, a result of Model B being made consistent with limitation in resources by the behavior in the system.

Model A also meets the counting rule but this is ensured by Say's Law being imposed on the system to eliminate a surplus equation. Moreover, as we discussed, Say's Law ensures that Model A is consistent with limitation in resources.

In sum, Say's Law rather than the behavior in Model A ensures consistency of the system with limitation in resources. This brings inconsistency into Model A, an inconsistency that will be resolved through Model B.

This, to review, is because the latter system will be made consistent with limitation in resources by the behavior in the system rather than by the non-behavioral Say's Law.

2.9 Summary

We have discussed how there is an inconsistency in the orthodox classical system, Model A, a system we use to represent orthodox microeconomic price systems. This inconsistency arises because Model A lacks an aspect to behavior that should ensure consistency of the system with limited resources.

Model A's inconsistency, however, will be resolved through Model B. This is because consistency of the latter system with limited resources will be ensured by the behavior in the system.

This will account for Model B reflecting the *general economic logic* that should characterize all price systems. However, this logic is suppressed in Model A.

This is because consistency of the latter system with limited resources is not ensured by the behavior in the system but is ensured by the non-behavioral Say's Law.

Hence while Model A reflects the *general logic* of price systems in reflecting consistency with limitation in resources, the system does not reflect the *general economic logic* of price systems. This is because consistency of the system with limited resources is not ensured by the behavior in the system.

We also discussed how the issue of Say's Law will be approached in the book through our dealing with the Law in terms of budget constraints.

To review, we shall establish that Model A is subject to an external budget constraint. This is a misused Say's Law in not being a true identity and it restricts the system to long-run states.

However, in resolving Model A's inconsistency through Model B, the external budget constraint form of the Law of Model A will be transformed into an internal budget constraint in Model B.

This budget constraint, in being internal to Model B, cannot possibly restrict the system to long-run states. This as we shall establish in Chapter 6, gives it the property of being a true identity form of the Law that hence cannot possibly restrict the system to long-run states.

We also discussed how Keynes rid his system of Model A's misused Say's Law through his use of aggregate demand and supply functions. However, this accounts for the microeconomics of the parts of his system that is based on these functions being suppressed.

On the other hand, we shall rid Model B of Model A's misused form of the Law in a manner that ensures that Model B is wholly microeconomic in character.

Finally, we discussed why the inconsistency of Model A was not uncovered in the literature. This is because the system *seems* to be consistent in that it meets the counting rule. However, hidden within the system is the economic inconsistency that we have uncovered and which we have described in detail.

Chapter 3

The Orthodox Classical Price System

3.1 Introduction

We shall now formally set out Model A, the system that we take to represent the orthodox classical price system.[3] There are a number of variants of this system in the literature.

However, there is a common element to them in that they are all characterized by what is referred to as an "homogeneity postulate." This is reflected in the systems' commodity demand and supply functions depending only on the relative commodity prices which are the ratios of the money prices of commodities.

Hence Model A, our version of the orthodox classical system, while differing in some ways from other forms of the system, will also be subject to this postulate.

We shall take Model A as a market system hence basing it on market demand and supply functions. As well, we shall initially develop it as a real system.

Next, we shall discuss how the system is inconsistent in that there is a surplus equation over the number of unknowns. Say's Law is then imposed on the system to eliminate this surplus equation.

However, while generally being taken to be consistent, we shall find that Model A reflects the economic inconsistency that we have uncovered; and we shall review this inconsistency and how it will be resolved.

3.2 Orthodox Microeconomic Price Systems

Orthodox microeconomic price systems such as Model A are based on market demand and supply functions that are intended to reflect the economic behavior of individuals and firms.

---

[3] On this system, see W.B. Hickman, "The Determinacy of Absolute Prices in Classical Economic Theory," *Econometrica*, XVlll (1950), pps. 9-20 and Patinkin, *op. cit.*, Ch. VIII.

This is in the sense that the functions show the quantities of commodities demanded and the quantities supplied at various prices, assuming that all other influences on these demands and supplies are fixed.

The latter include the tastes and preferences of individuals and firms as well as their resources. Moreover, population and the state of technology are held fixed. There is next the question of consistency of the systems.

Behavior in the systems must, of course, meet the well-known axioms or conditions for consistency and rationality of behavior set out in the literature.[4]

We also discussed in Chapter 1.1, how economists ensure consistency of orthodox price systems such as Model A; and they use a "counting rule" to ensure such consistency.

This is through equating the number of independent equations and unknowns in the systems. There are various qualifications to this counting rule as economists have pointed out.

However, we also discussed how economists generally take equality between the number of independent equations and unknowns of a system to mean that it is reasonable to assume that the system is consistent.

Consistency, when ensured by a system meeting the counting rule implies that one set of variables can simultaneously satisfy every equation in the system.

As well, we pointed out that economists also usually assume that there exists only one set of variables that simultaneously satisfies every equation of a system. With this as background, let us now focus on the orthodox classical system, Model A.

This system will allow us to illustrate how consistency of price systems is usually ensured along orthodox lines. Yet we shall find that Model A is characterized by the economic inconsistency that we have uncovered.

This inconsistency, to review, arises because Model A lacks an aspect to behavior that should ensure consistency of the system with limited resources.

----

[4] On these axioms or conditions for consistency and rationality of behavior see J.M. Henderson and R.E. Quandt, *Microeconomic Theory: A Mathematical Approach* (New York, 1958), Chs. 2 and 3. Also, Vickrey, *op. cit.*, where Ch. 2 considers the consumer and Ch. 4 considers the firm.

3.3 A Preliminary Form Of The Orthodox Classical System

We shall set out Model A by basing it on a preliminary form of the system, Model A', that is shown below. This is a preliminary form of Model A since it will have to be adapted to ensure that it reflects rational behavior:

Model A'

1. $D_j \equiv F(p_j)$

2. $S_j \equiv G(p_j)$

3. $E(p_j) = 0$

Model A' is a system in which there are n commodities. There is also a fixed supply of outside money which is assumed to be a neutral medium-of-exchange. Hence we define commodities to exclude money.

We use the variables D_j and S_j to denote the quantities of commodities demanded and supplied, respectively, $j=1,2,3,...,n$. There are also n money prices of commodities, denoted by p_j . Expressions (1) and (2) are the system's commodity demand and supply functions, respectively.

Functions (1) indicate that the quantities of commodities demanded, the D_j depend on the money prices of these commodities which we denote by p_j . While functions (2) indicate that the quantities of commodities supplied, the S_j also depend on the p_j .

These demand and supply functions also depend on the tastes and preferences of individuals and firms and on their resources as well as on the other variables referred to earlier. All of these variables, however, are assumed to be fixed hence we have not shown them explicitly.

Equations (3) are the commodity excess-demand equations of Model A'. They are derived as usual from the commodity demand and supply functions. This is by taking the differences between the quantity demanded and supplied in each market across the system.

These differences or excess-demands, like the quantities demanded and supplied, hence also depend on the money prices, the p_j . Model A' as we pointed out is a preliminary form of the orthodox classical system, Model A. This is because Model A' has to be adapted to ensure that it reflects rational behavior.

Let us follow the literature and adapt Model A' to bring rational behavior into this system which is through imposing the "homogeneity postulate" on the system.

3.4 Rational Behavior In Model A

Rational behavior requires that the demands and supplies of commodities depend only on real variables as opposed to nominal money variables. Real price variables are relative prices which are derived by taking the ratios of the money prices.

We have, however, made the demands and supplies of commodities in Model A' depend on the money prices. These money prices, however, are nominal money variables rather than real variables.

This is because a proportionate change in all money prices, which is a change in the price level, will leave the real or relative prices unchanged. This means that were behavior made to depend on the money prices, behavior would change in response to such a nominal monetary change.

This would reflect irrational behavior or what is referred to as "money illusion" since the real or relative prices have not changed.[5] Hence we shall adapt Model A' to make behavior depend only on the relative prices to ensure that behavior is rational in the system.

Model A' is characterized by n money prices of commodities. We next take the ratios of these money prices to arrive at $(n-1)$ price ratios or relative prices which we shall denote z.

We next form Model A below by re-writing Model A' to make the quantities of commodities demanded and supplied depend on the relative prices, that is, on the z.

We thereby impose what is referred to as the "homogeneity postulate" on the system in order to introduce rational behavior into the system. This behavior rids the system of "money illusion."

---

[5] On the orthodox concept of "money illusion" see, for example, Patinkin, *op. cit.*, pps. 174-76.

Following this approach, we arrive at Model A below which we take to take to represent the orthodox classical system:

Model A

4. $D_j \equiv F_j [z]$

5. $S_j \equiv G_j [z]$

6. $E_j [z] = 0$

Model A as we noted is characterized by the "homogeneity postulate" which is reflected in our making quantities demanded (supplied) depend on the relative prices.[6] This as discussed earlier, is a main reason why we take Model A to represent the orthodox classical system.

Behavior in Model A is rational in the sense of depending only on the real or relative prices, the z, as opposed to the money prices. This is reflected in Model A's demand functions, functions (4), making the quantities of commodities demanded depend only on the relative prices.

As well, the system's supply functions, functions (5), also make the quantities of commodities supplied depend only on the relative prices. Model A's demand and supply functions then lead to the system's excess-demand equations, equations (6).

These latter equations show that the system's excess commodity demands also depend only on the relative prices. Let us now consider consistency of the system following orthodox analysis.

There are expressions implicit in Model A reflecting the demand and supply of money flows. These are derived from the money prices and the quantities of commodities demanded and supplied.

However, these expressions are dependent on the commodity equations hence they cannot be the basis for an equilibrium constraint on the system.

This means that since there are n commodities in Model A, there are n demand and n supply functions in each of (4) and (5). As a result, there are also n excess-demand equations in (6).

---

[6] On the "homogeneity postulate" see also Patinkin, *op. cit.*, pps. 174-76.

On the other hand, the unknowns to be determined are the relative prices which are only $(n-1)$ number. Hence the number of equations exceeds the number of unknowns which means that the system may be overdetermined and inconsistent.

That is, there are too many restrictions in the form of equations compared to variables that are imposed on the system hence these restrictions cannot all be met simultaneously.

There is, however, a further element to be brought into Model A which will eliminate the system's surplus equation to ensure consistency of the system.

That is, to ensure that the number of independent equations equals the number of variables to be determined. This element is Say's Law to which we have already referred but which we shall now consider in more detail.

3.5 Say's Law

Model A is also characterized by Say's Law which is an identity between the aggregate demand and supply of commodities. [7] Economists arrive at this identity form of the Law of the classical system in various ways.

However, most commonly, it is held that the classical economists assumed that individuals and firms sell commodities only to buy other commodities. That is, commodities are exchanged only for other commodities.

This implies that the aggregate demand for commodities (ad) is identical to the aggregate supply (as) of commodities which is Say's Law. We show the Say's Law identity below:

7. $\qquad ad \equiv as$

This identity is arrived at by the quantities of commodities demanded and the quantities supplied being measured in a common unit and summed to derive the aggregate demand and supply variables in (7).

Economists then use the Say's Law identity to eliminate the surplus equation in Model A to ensure equality of the number

---

[7] On Say's Law see J.B. Say, *A Treatise on Political Economy*, trans. by C.R. Prinsep (1834), pps.138-139. See also the paper by G.S Becker and W.J. Baumol, "The Classical Monetary Theory: The Outcome of the Discussion," *Economica*, XIX (1952), pps. 356-7.

of independent equations and unknowns in the system. However, we shall establish in Chapter 5.2 that the Law ensures consistency of the system with limited resources.

This, however, as we discussed earlier, is an invalid use of Say's Law which brings a misused form of the Law into Model A that restricts the system to long-run states. Let us review why Model A reflects an incorrect or misused form of Say's Law.

Say's Law is a true identity in being simply a description of the overall output or income of a system alternatively as aggregate demand and aggregate supply. Hence no substantive role should be attributed to it.

Yet the Law in Model A as we shall discuss in Chapter 5.2 is given the substantive role of ensuring consistency of the system with limited resources. This means that the Law in Model A is a misused form of the Law since it is not a true identity.

This is because the Law in being a true identity should not be given the substantive role described of ensuring consistency of Model A with limited resources.

This, as we shall now discuss, brings a misused Say's Law into Model A; and it is this misused Say's Law rather than Say's Law proper that restricts the system to long-run states.

Economists in setting out Model A write Say's Law as an identity. However, this identity is misused in Model A in being given the substantive role described.

This is why we concluded that there is a misused form of the Law in Model A; since a true identity form of the Law should not be given the substantive role described.

In sum, it is true as Keynes held that Model A is restricted by Say's Law to long-run states. *However, this is due to a misused Say's Law that is imposed on the system.*

Hence the solution to the issue of Say's Law restricting Model A to long-run states is to bring a correctly used Say's Law into the system, a form of the Law that is a true identity. This is the approach followed in this book.

Keynes, in contrast, rid his system wholly of the Law rather than bringing a correct form of the Law into his system. This is through Keynes forming aggregate demand and supply functions.

These allow the aggregate demand and supply of commodities to diverge to rid his system of the Law. However, these aggregative functions suppress the microeconomics of the parts of the Keynesian system that are based on such functions.

In contrast, we shall rid Model B of Model A's misused Say's Law through microeconomic analysis. This will account for Model B being wholly microeconomic in character.

3.6 Introducing Money Into Model A

Model A, the orthodox classical system appears below:

$$\textbf{Model A}$$

4. $\quad D_j \equiv F_j[z]$

5. $\quad S_j \equiv G_j[z]$

6. $\quad E_j[z] = 0$

Model A is a wholly real system since money and hence money prices or the price level are missing from it. However, we shall follow the literature and bring money and money prices into the system. This is by complementing the system with a long-run Cambridge cash-balance equation which appears below:

8. $\quad K[p_1 X_1 + p_2 X_2 + \cdots p_n X_n] = M$

The variable K represents the proportion of their money income that individuals and firms hold as a cash balance. We also assume that these balances are held only for transactions purposes. That is, to offset any possible lack of synchronization between payments and receipts.

Next, overall money income in Model A is represented by the term $[p_1 X_1 + p_2 X_2 + \cdots p_n X_n]$ where $X_1, X_2, \ldots, X_n$ are the system's equilibrium quantities of commodities, each of which is multiplied by the appropriate price.

As we discussed, the variable K is the proportion of their money income that individuals and firms hold as a cash balance.

Hence the whole expression to the left of the equality sign in (8) is the demand for money to hold for transactions purposes. While M to the right of (8) is the given supply of nominal money.

We next substitute the equilibrium quantities of commodities and the equilibrium relative prices from Model A into condition (8). This allows us to solve for the individual money prices or the price level from the latter condition.

As a result, we strictly followed the orthodox literature in forming Model A in two parts: First, a real part that is reflected in Model A then a monetary part that is reflected in the Cambridge equation.

Next we complemented Model A with the Cambridge equation to bring money and the price level into Model A to form a monetary version of the system.

Patinkin, however, has shown that money and the price level are not satisfactorily integrated into the monetary form of Model A. This is readily confirmed.

Let us move the price level of the monetary Model A from equilibrium by making an equiproportionate change in the individual money prices. This throws the money equation (8) out of equilibrium.

This should on account of Walras Law, which reflects the system's budget constraint, should also throw the commodity markets out of equilibrium. However, the commodity markets remain in equilibrium.

This is because they depend only on the relative prices which are unaffected by the change in the price level. As a result, no commodity market comes out of equilibrium to bring the price level back to equilibrium.

In sum, as Patinkin held, the price level of Model A is indeterminate with the system hence being invalidly dichotomized into real and monetary parts. As well, Walras Law which we shall consider in detail later, is violated in the system.

Patinkin held that these problems with Model A are caused by the system's "homogeneity postulate." However, we shall establish that these problems stem from the inconsistency we have uncovered in the system.

As a result, in resolving Model A's inconsistency through Model B, we shall rid the latter system of Model A's "homogeneity postulate" and hence of the problems of Model A we described that are caused by this postulate.

This as will be discussed in Chapter 7 will account for Model B being rid of the price level indeterminacy and an invalid real-monetary dichotomy that characterize Model A, problems brought out by Patinkin.

3.7 Review Of The Inconsistency In Orthodox Price Systems

Price systems are necessarily *subject* to limitation in resources. Hence the systems reflect consistency with limitation in resources.

That is, the quantities of commodities demanded and supplied in price systems should each sum to the systems' limited or given resources to hence exhaust these resources.

However, Model A, the orthodox classical system, lacks an aspect to behavior that should ensure consistency of the system with limitation in resources. Consistency of the system with limited resources as we discussed, is then ensured by the non-behavioral Say's Law.

This brings inconsistency into the system since consistency of the system with limited resources should be ensured by the behavior in the system. Let us now consider Model B, our revised form of Model A.

We shall incorporate into Model B through the system's functions, an aspect to behavior that ensures consistency of the system with limitation in resources. Hence we shall rid Model B of Model A's inconsistency.

Clearly, also, Model B will be rid of Say's Law that ensures consistency of Model A with limited resources; since as discussed, consistency of Model B with limited resources will be ensured by the behavior in the system rather than by Say's Law as in Model A.

Moreover, since Say's Law restricts Model A to long-run states Model B, in being rid of the Law, will not be restricted in this way.

3.8 Summary

Model A, the orthodox classical price system, was set out in this chapter. This is a real system that is characterized by the "homogeneity postulate" that makes quantities of commodities demanded and supplied depend on the relative commodity prices.

We then discussed how the system is initially inconsistent in that there is a surplus equation over the number of unknowns. Say's Law is then imposed on the system to eliminate this surplus equation.

However, Model A while seeming to be consistent in meeting the counting rule is yet characterized by the economic inconsistency we have uncovered in the system.

This inconsistency, to review arises because Model A lacks an aspect to behavior that should ensure consistency of the system with limitation in resources. Consistency of the system with limited resources is then ensured by the non-behavioral Say's Law.

This brings inconsistency into the system since consistency of the system with limited resources should be ensured by the behavior in the system.

However, we shall incorporate into Model B through the system's functions, an aspect to behavior that ensures consistency of the system with limitation in resources.

This will account for Model B being rid of Model A's inconsistency and of basic problems that stem from this inconsistency. Finally, in resolving Model A's inconsistency, we shall be able to integrate microeconomic and macroeconomic analysis, see Chapter 11.

Chapter 4

Issues Concerning The Orthodox Classical System

4.1 Introduction

Keynes held in the *General Theory* that Say's Law accounts for the orthodox classical system, which we represent by Model A, being restricted to describing long-run, full-employment states.

We shall find that this problem with Model A that was brought out by Keynes arises because of the inconsistency we have uncovered in the system. Hence this problem with Model A can only be satisfactorily resolved by resolving this inconsistency.

This will be accomplished through Model B by our bringing into this system an aspect to behavior that ensures consistency of the system with limited resources. This is an aspect to behavior that is missing from Model A which accounts for the inconsistency in the system.

Consequently, we shall rid Model B of the inconsistency of Model A that is the cause of the system being restricted by Say's Law to long-run states.

This as will be discussed in Chapter 6 will account for Model B being characterized by a true identity form of Say's Law that hence cannot possibly restrict the system to long-run states.

4.2 Keynes' Criticism Of The Classical System

Keynes in the *General Theory* imputed an identity form of Say's Law to the classical system.[8] This is a form of the Law that takes the aggregate demand for commodities to be identical to the aggregate supply.

Model A which we use to represent the orthodox classical system, is characterized by this form of Say's Law. Next, the Law is imposed on Model A to eliminate a surplus equation from the system.

---

[8] J.M.Keynes, *The General Theory Of Employment, Interest And Money* (New York, 1936), esp. Chs. 2 and 3.

Hence Say's Law allows us to solve Model A for the system's equilibrium prices and quantities. Moreover, the Law as will now be discussed, allows for the existence of a long-run market equilibrating process that clears every market in the system.

Say's Law, to review, puts the aggregate demand for commodities identical to the aggregate supply. Hence if there are excess demands anywhere in the system, these are matched by an equal excess supply elsewhere in the system.

Economists drawing on long-run analysis then conclude that the relative prices will instantaneously adjust to eliminate this disequilibrium in the various markets of the system without changing overall output or income.

This is a long-run, full-employment overall output or income although there will be frictional unemployment, a consequence of job search.

Keynes, however, formed a short-run or macroeconomic system where general unemployment can occur; and to do so, he had to abandon Say's Law and the perfectly flexible classical price mechanism we described that is implied by the Law.

Keynes then showed that there were various reasons why aggregate demand may be deficient to cause aggregate supply or overall output to fall below a full-employment level. Hence Keynes regarded his system as being more general than the orthodox classical system.

This is because the Keynesian system can describe short-run states that are characterized by general unemployment. On the other hand, the orthodox classical system is restricted by Say's Law to describing long-run, full-employment states.

This has been a review of Keynes' claim that Model A is restricted by Say's Law to long-run states; and we shall find that Model A is indeed restricted by Say's Law long-run states.

However, in contrast to Keynes, we shall establish that this is because Model A is characterized by a misused Say's Law. This misused Say's Law enters Model A as a result of the inconsistency we uncover in the system; and it is this misused Say's Law that restricts Model A to long-run states.

Hence in ridding Model B of Model A's inconsistency, we shall bring a correctly used form of the Law into Model B. This we shall find in Chapter 6.4 is a true identity that hence cannot possibly restrict the system to long-run states or cause other problems commonly attribute to the Law. Let us review why Model A reflects a misused form of Say's Law.

4.3 There Is A Misused Form Of Say's Law In Model A

Say's Law is widely taken following Keynes to account for the orthodox classical system, which we represent by Model A being restricted to describing long-run, full-employment states.

However, we shall find that this is due to the inconsistency that we uncover in the system. This inconsistency, to review, arises because Model A's functions do not ensure that the system is consistent with limitation in resources.

That is, Model A's functions do not ensure that the quantities of commodities demanded (supplied) each sum to the system's limited resources to hence exhaust these resources. This results in Model A being characterized by a surplus equation over the number of unknowns.

Say's Law is then imposed on the system to eliminate this surplus equation. Moreover, the Law as we shall establish in Chapter 5.2, ensures consistency of the system with limited resources.

This explains why we concluded that there is a misused form of the Law in Model A; since a correct form of the Law, in being a true identity, should not be given the substantive role of ensuring consistency of the system with limited resources.

However, in resolving Model A's economic inconsistency through Model B, we shall find as will be discussed in Chapter 6.3 that the latter system automatically meets the counting rule. Hence we do not need Say's Law to ensure that Model B is consistent by eliminating a surplus equation from the system as is the case with Model A.

This rids Model B of Model A's misused Say's Law which is not a true identity and which restricts the system to long-run states. This will result in Model B being characterized by a true form of the Law.

This is a form of the Law which, as will be discussed in Chapter 6.4, is a true identity since it is solely a descriptive device in the system.

As a result, Model B's Say's Law cannot possibly restrict the system to long-run states. Instead, Model B will describe long-run states on account of the behavior in the system rather than on account of Say's Law.

4.4 Remarks On The Restriction Of Model A By Say's Law To Long-Run States

We discussed in Section 4.2 of the chapter how Keynes held that Model A is restricted to long-run states by Say's Law. True, Model A is restricted to long-run states by Say's Law. However, as we established, this is because the Law in the system is a misused form of the Law.

Were it a correct form of the Law, it could not possibly restrict Model A to long-run states. This is because a correct form of the Law is a true identity that is simply a descriptive device in a system. Hence it can have no substantive influence in a system.

Economists clearly recognize that Say's Law is a true identity in that they create it by describing the overall output or income of Model A alternatively as aggregate demand and aggregate supply. Hence the Law is simply a descriptive device in the system which explains why it is a true identity.

Economists, however, do not ensure that the Law is indeed a true identity when they write Model A. This is because as discussed earlier, the Law in Model A is given the substantive role of ensuring consistency of the system with limited resources.

Hence the form of the Law that actually characterizes Model A, in having such a substantive role, is not a true identity. This means that it is not a correctly used Say's Law; and it is this incorrect or misused Say's Law that restricts Model A to long-run states.

However, as we shall discuss in Chapter 6.4, we shall bring a correctly used Say's Law into Model B. This is a form of the Law that is a true identity hence it cannot possible restrict the system to long-run states.

This means that we shall resolve through Model B, the problem of Model A being restricted to long-run states by Say's Law. Moreover, we shall find that Model B's correct form of the Law is a budget constraint of relevance to microeconomics.

This is because individual quantities of commodities emerge from this budget constraint. This accounts for Model B being wholly microeconomic in character.

In sum, Model A and Model B are both long-run microeconomic systems. However, Model B unlike Model A is not restricted to long-run states by a misused Say's Law.

Keynes also rid his system of Model A's incorrect or misused form of the Law but this was through Keynes allowing the aggregate demand and supply of commodities in his system to diverge.

However, as we discussed in Chapter 2.5, Keynes' approach to ridding his system of Model A's incorrect or misused Say's Law suppresses the microeconomics of the parts of his system that are based on his aggregate demand and supply functions.

Whereas we shall rid Model B of Model A's incorrect or misused Say's Law while ensuring that Model B is wholly microeconomic in character as will be discussed in Chapter 9.4.

4.5 Further Remarks On The Restriction Of Model A By Say's Law To Long-Run States

We have discussed how Keynes held that Model A is restricted to long-run states by Say's Law. This problem with Model A that was brought out by Keynes is a *symptom or consequence* of the inconsistency that we uncover in Model A. Hence this problem can only be satisfactorily resolved through resolving this inconsistency.

This will be accomplished through Model B by our basing the latter system on a new type of demand and supply functions that will be set out in Chapters 5 and 6. As a result, Model B, unlike Model A, will not be restricted by the Law to long-run states.

This means that Model B is a generalization of Model A whereas the Keynesian system bypasses the inconsistency of Model A. Hence the Keynesian system is an alternative to Model A.

Let us discuss in more detail why Model B is a generalization of Model A whereas the Keynesian system is an alternative to Model A.

Keynes held that Model A is restricted to long-run states by Say's Law. However, we show that this is because the Law in Model A is a misused Say's Law in not being a true identity; and it is this misused Say's Law, rather than a true form of the Law, that restricts the system to long-run states.

Hence to resolve this problem with Model A, we need to bring a correctly-used Say's Law into the system. This is the course we follow in this book through Model B. This will confirm that Model B is a generalization of Model A.

Keynes, in contrast, wholly rid his system of Model A's misused Say's Law while leaving Model A untouched and hence still characterized by a misused Say's Law. This reflects how the Keynesian system is an alternative to Model A.

In sum, Keynes formed a system that is an alternative to Model A. This is reflected in Keynes leaving Model A untouched and hence still characterized by the problem of being restricted by Say's Law to long-run states.

On the other hand, Model B as we discussed is a generalization of Model A. Let go further into what accounts for this difference between Model B and the Keynesian system.

4.6 Remarks On The New Approach To Price Systems

Model B is based on an approach that focuses on the *general economic logic* that should underlie all price systems rather than on the specific forms of behavior of individual systems. This is through our focusing on how consistency with limitation in resources is to be ensured in the systems.

Our pursuing this issue of how consistency of price systems with limitation in resources is to be ensured accounts for our uncovering and resolving through Model B, the inconsistency we have described that characterizes Model A, the orthodox classical system.

This allows us to arrive through Model B at a very general approach to price systems. This is because in dealing with the issue of consistency of price systems with limitation in resources, we deal with the *general logic* that should characterize all price systems.

Moreover, we shall arrive through Model B at a correct approach to ensuring consistency of price systems with limitation in resources.

This is reflected in Model B being made consistent with limitation in resources by the behavior in the system. This accounts for Model B reflecting the *general economic logic* of price systems.

On the other hand, as we shall establish in Chapter 5.2, Model A is made consistent with limitation in resources as a result of Say's Law being imposed on the system to eliminate a surplus equation.

Hence while Model A reflects the *general logic* of price systems in reflecting consistency with limitation in resources, Model A does not reflect the *general economic logic* of price systems. This is because consistency with limitation in resources is not ensured by the behavior in the system.

This brings inconsistency into Model A, an inconsistency that will be resolved through Model B; since consistency of this latter system with limited resources will be ensured by the behavior in the system.

Clearly, the Keynesian system, unlike Model B, does not deal with the general economic logic that should characterize all price systems. Instead, the Keynesian system deals with the specific forms of behavior of the system.

Hence the Keynesian system cannot possibly resolve the inconsistency of Model A since this requires bringing into the latter system the general economic logic of price systems. This also explains why Keynes could not satisfactorily resolve the problem with Model A that he brought up.

Namely, the problem of Model A being restricted to long-run states by Say's Law. This is because to satisfactorily resolve this problem with Model A requires that we resolve the inconsistency we have uncovered in the system.

This will be accomplished through Model B by our bringing into the latter system an aspect to behavior that is missing from Model A. This, to review, is an aspect to behavior that ensures consistency of Model B with limited resources.

Consequently, Model B is a generalization of Model A rather than being an alternative to Model A as is the case with the Keynesian system.

Hence this latter system, in being an alternatives to Model A, cannot possibly get to the root cause of the problem with Model A that accounts for the system being restricted by Say's Law to long-run states.

This is because this problem stems from the inconsistency that we uncover in Model A, an inconsistency that is bypassed by the Keynesian system but which will be resolved through Model B.

4.7 The Keynesian System Deals Only With A Symptom Of The Inconsistency Of Model A

We have discussed how the Keynesian system is an alternative to Model A whereas Model B is a generalization of Model A. This may also be established in the following way.

Keynes showed that Model A is restricted to long-run states by Say's Law. Next, Keynes approached this problem of Model A through his short-run or macroeconomic system.

However, as we noted earlier in the chapter, this problem of Model A being restricted by the Law to long-run states is a symptom or consequence of the inconsistency in Model A uncovered in this book.

Hence Keynes in approaching this problem of Model A through his system, dealt with this symptom or consequence of the inconsistency of Model A that we have uncovered rather than with this inconsistency itself.

However, to satisfactorily resolve the problem with Model A that was brought out by Keynes, we need to resolve the underlying inconsistency in Model A since this inconsistency is the cause of this problem.

This is the approach to this problem followed in this book through Model B. This is because through this system, we shall resolve the underlying inconsistency in Model A that is the cause of the latter system being restricted by Say's Law to long-run states. Clearly, this accounts for Model B being a generalization of Model A.

Keynes, however, bypassed in his system the underlying inconsistency in Model A that is the cause of the system being restricted by Say's Law to long-run states. This explains why the Keynesian system is an alternative to Model A whereas Model B is a generalization of Model A since Model B is rid of the inconsistency of Model A.

4.8 Summary

Keynes held in the *General Theory* that Say's Law accounts for the orthodox classical system, which we represent by Model A, being restricted by Say's Law to describing long-run, full-employment states.

We shall find that this problem with Model A stems from the inconsistency we uncover in the system. However, we shall rid Model B of this inconsistency of Model A.

This will be accomplished by our bringing into Model B an aspect to behavior that ensures consistency of the system with limitation in resources, an aspect to behavior that is missing from Model A .

Consequently, through Model B we shall generalize Model A which will rid Model B of the inconsistency of Model A. This will also result in Model B, unlike Model A, not being restricted by Say's Law to long-run states.

In contrast, Keynes in his system bypassed the inconsistency of Model A. This is reflected in Keynes leaving

Model A untouched and hence still characterized by the problem of being restricted by Say's Law to long-run states.

In sum, Keynes formed a system that is an alternative to Model A. Whereas we rid Model B of Model A's inconsistency with Model B hence being a generalization of Model A.

This as will be discussed in Chapter 6, will result in Model B being rid in a satisfactory manner of the key problem with Model A that was brought out by Keynes. That is, the problem of Model A being restricted by Say's Law to long-run states.

Chapter 5

Generalizing Orthodox Demand And Supply Functions

5.1 Introduction

We discussed at the outset of the book how we should approach price systems by first uncovering the *general economic logic* that should characterize all price systems. Then we should ensure that particular systems conform to this logic.

Clearly, this approach to price systems will bring a unity to the systems, a unity that is missing from orthodox price systems. This is reflected, for example, in orthodox microeconomic and macroeconomic systems being dichotomized.

5.2 Consistency With Limitation In Resources In The Orthodox Classical System

Model A, the orthodox classical system, appears again below:

Model A

4. $\quad D_j \equiv F_j[z]$

5. $\quad S_j \equiv G_j[z]$

6. $\quad E_j[z] = 0$

We have discussed how Say's Law which was set out in Chapter 3.5 is imposed on Model A to eliminate a surplus equation from the system. This identity is shown again below:

7. $\quad\quad\quad\quad\quad ad \equiv as$

We derive the aggregate demand (ad) and aggregate supply (as) variables in expression (7) by measuring the individual quantities of commodities demanded (supplied) in a common unit. We then sum these quantities to derive the aggregate demand and supply variables in expression (7).

38

All price systems are necessarily subject to limitation in resources. Consequently, we should be able to find a variable in Model A that we may take as reflecting the system's limited resources.

We shall proceed by taking the aggregate supply of commodities (*as*) in the Say's Law identity (7) to reflect Model A's limited resources which we shall denote by W. This variable also reflects the system's long-run overall output or income.

However, we shall now deal with W as reflecting Model A's limited resources but later in the book, we shall deal with W in the sense of also reflecting the system's overall flow of output or income.

As discussed, the variable W reflects the aggregate supply of commodities. Hence W, on account of Say's Law, also reflects the aggregate demand for commodities.

Now the aggregate demand for commodities reflects the sum of individual quantities demanded while the aggregate supply of commodities reflects the sum of individual quantities supplied.

Consequently, since aggregate demand and supply of commodities each equal W, the individual quantities demanded and supplied each sum to W.

This reflects how the variable W, and hence Say's Law from which we derived this variable, ensures consistency of the system with limited resources.

However, this approach to ensuring consistency of Model A with limited resources is invalid and brings inconsistency into the system. This is because consistency of Model A with limited resources should be ensured by the behavior in the system rather than by Say's Law.

We shall now sketch how Model B will be rid of Model A's inconsistency. This will be accomplished by our ensuring that consistency of Model B with limited resources is ensured by the behavior in the system rather than by Say's Law..

This will account for Model B reflecting the general *economic logic* that should characterize all price systems, a logic that is missing from Model A.

5.3 The Rationale Of Model B's Demand And Supply Functions

Model A, the orthodox classical system makes *quantities* of commodities demanded (supplied) depend on the relative prices.

However, to form Model B, we shall make *relative* quantities of commodities demanded (supplied) depend on the relative prices. Let us first set out the rationale that underlies Model B's functions.

We shall establish that as the relative price change, quantities demanded (supplied) will adjust in a relative manner to always exhaust the system's limited resources. Consequently, consistency with limitation in resources will be ensured in Model B by the behavior in the system.

This means that Model B will be rid of Model A's inconsistency. This inconsistency, to review, arises because consistency of Model A with limited resources is ensured by the non-behavioral Say's Law rather than by the behavior in the system.

We shall now provide a sketch of how we shall write Model B's functions which will be set out in full detail in the next chapter.

In setting out these functions, we need to assume that the variable W, that reflects the system's limited flow of resources, and quantities of commodities demanded (supplied) are all measured in a similar common unit.

5.4 Forming Model B's Demand And Supply Functions

To form Model B's demand and supply functions, we require new sets of functions, to be called "internal functions." These internal functions appear below:

9. $\quad r \equiv f(z)$
10. $\quad s \equiv g(z)$

Functions (9) make the ratios of the quantities of commodities demanded, the r, depend on the relative prices, the z. While functions (10) make the ratios of the quantities of commodities supplied, the s, also depend on the relative prices, on the z.

We shall now discuss how these functions together with the variable W which reflects Model B limited flow of resources, provide the basis for the Model B's demand and supply functions.

We shall take W and functions $f(z)$ as the independent elements in Model B's demand functions. Next, functions $f(z)$ operate on W to determine relative quantities of commodities demanded as functions of the relative prices. These quantities adjust in a relative manner to always exhaust W.

These relative quantities of commodities demanded then become the dependent variables in Model B's demand functions. Let us now consider Model B's supply functions.

We shall take W and functions $g(z)$ as the independent elements in Model B's supply functions. Next, functions $g(z)$ operate on W to determine relative quantities of commodities supplied as functions of the relative prices.

These quantities adjust in a relative manner to always exhaust W. these relative quantities then become the dependent variables in Model B's supply functions.

In sum, consistency with limited resources is ensured in Model B by the behavior in the system. This is because relative quantities of commodities demanded (supplied) in the system depend on the relative prices.

Hence as the relative prices change, quantities demanded (supplied) adjust in a relative manner to always exhaust the system's limited resources W. That is, the behavior in Model B ensures consistency of the system with limited resources.

This means that Model B is rid of the inconsistency of Model A. This inconsistency, to review, arises because consistency of Model A with limited resources is ensured by Say's Law rather than by the behavior in the system as is the case with Model B.

Clearly, Model B will also be rid of Say's Law that ensures consistency of Model A with limited resources but which restricts the system to long-run states.

This is because as we established, consistency of Model B with limited resources will be ensured by the behavior in the system rather than by Say's Law as in Model A.

Yet as we shall discuss in the following chapter, Model B will be characterized by the Law but a correctly used form of the Law. This we shall find is a true identity that hence cannot possibly restrict the system to long-run states.

5.5 Summary

We discussed at the outset of the book how we should approach price systems by first uncovering the *general economic logic* that should characterize all price systems. Then we should write particular systems to conform to this logic.

This is the approach to price systems suggested in this book, an approach that brings a unity to the systems. This is because all systems, while reflecting different forms of behavior, will be characterized by this general economic logic. Whereas such a unity is missing from orthodox price systems which is reflected, for example, in orthodox microeconomic and macroeconomic systems being dichotomized.

Next, we established earlier that the general economic logic of price systems is reflected in consistency of the systems with limited resources being ensured by the behavior in the systems.

However, we also established that Model A lacks an aspect to behavior that should ensure consistency of the system with limited resources. This brought inconsistency into Model A since consistency of the system with limited resources should be ensured by the behavior in the system.

We then provided a sketch of how we shall write Model B's functions so that the functions and hence the behavior in the system ensures consistency the system with limited resources.

This is because relative quantities of commodities demanded (supplied) in Model B will depend on the relative prices. Hence as the relative prices change, quantities demanded (supplied) adjust in a relative manner to always exhaust the system's limited resources.

That is, consistency of Model B with limited resources will be ensured by the behavior in the system, Model B hence being rid of Model A's inconsistency.

Consequently, Model B's functions while reflecting the behavior of this particular system will also incorporate into the system the *general economic logic* that should underlie all price systems.

Moreover, Model B will be rid of Say's Law that characterizes Model A. This is because the Law ensures consistency of Model A with limited resources. Whereas we have established that consistency of Model B with limited resources will be ensured by the behavior in the system.

Chapter 6

Revision Of The Orthodox Classical System

6.1 Introduction

We described earlier the inconsistency we have uncovered in Model A, the orthodox classical price system. This inconsistency, to review, arises in Model A because the system lacks an aspect to behavior that should ensure consistency of the system with limited resources. Hence the system does not reflect the general *economic* logic that should underlie all price systems.

However, we shall rid Model B of the inconsistency of Model A by basing Model B on the new type of functions that were described in the previous chapter. These new functions will incorporate into Model B, behavior that ensures consistency of the system with limitation in resources.

Consequently, Model B in reflecting behavior that ensures consistency of the system with limited resources, will be rid of the inconsistency of Model A. Moreover, as we shall establish in the chapter, this will account for Model B being rid of Say's Law that restricts Model A to long-run states.

6.2 The Revised Classical System

Model B our revised classical system, like Model A, is also a long-run, microeconomic system. However, the systems differ significantly. This is because we approach our new systems, which we represent by Model B, by pursuing the issue of how consistency of the systems with limitation in resources is to be ensured.

This approach is based on our bringing into Model B through the system's functions, an aspect to the behavior of individuals and firms that ensures consistency of the system with limited resources.

However, this aspect to behavior is missing from Model A which accounts for the inconsistency we have uncovered in the system. We shall resolve Model A's inconsistency through

Model B, our revised classical system, which we shall now set out in detail.

As in Model A, there are also n quantities of commodities in Model B. As well, we shall continue to denote the quantities of commodities demanded by D_j and the quantities supplied by S_j, where $j=1,2,3,...,n$.

Moreover, as in Model A, the quantities of commodities demanded and supplied in Model B, the D_j and S_j, are quantities that enter the markets of the system. That is, Model A and Model B are both market systems.

We shall also use the variable z to denote the relative commodity prices of Model B as was done in the case of Model A. These relative prices, to review, are derived by taking the ratios of the n money prices in the system.

We have discussed in the previous chapter how we shall ensure that quantities of commodities in Model B are relative quantities.

These quantities will then adjust in a relative manner as the relative prices change, to exhaust the system's limited resources. Hence consistency of the system with limited resources will be ensured by the behavior in the system.

We show below Model B's internal functions that were set out in the previous chapter:

9. $\quad r \equiv f(z)$

10. $\quad s \equiv g(z)$

Functions (9) make the ratios of the quantities of commodities demanded, the r, depend on the relative prices, the z. While functions (10) make the ratios of the quantities of commodities supplied, the s, depend on the relative prices, that is, on the z.

We next use the variable W that reflects Model B's limited flow of resources and functions $f(z)$ and $g(z)$ to form Model B's demand and supply functions, namely, functions (11) and (12) below.

Functions (11) and (12) then lead to the system's excess-demand equations, namely, equations (13). Below is the complete

Model B, which is our revised classical system:

Model B

11. $\quad D_j \equiv F_j' \big[W, f(z) \big]$

12. $\quad S_j \equiv G_j' \big[W, g(z) \big]$

13. $\quad E_j' \big[W \{ f(z) - g(z) \} = 0 \big] = 0$

Model B's demand functions (11) are shown to depend on W and functions $f(z)$. The latter functions determine the ratios of quantities demanded as function of the relative prices, the z.

Next, following our analysis of the previous chapter, functions $f(z)$ operate on W to determine relative quantities of commodities demanded as functions of the relative prices.

That is, quantities demanded, the D_j in (11), are relative quantities that adjust in a relative manner as the z change to always exhaust W. There is a generally similar analysis on the supply side.

Model B's supply functions (12) show quantities of commodities supplied, the S_j, as depending on W and functions $g(z)$. The latter functions determine the *ratios* of quantities supplied as functions of the relative prices, the z.

Next, again following our analysis of the previous chapter, functions $g(z)$ operate on W to determine relative quantities of commodities supplied.

Hence quantities supplied, the S_j in (12), are relative quantities that adjust in a relative manner as the z change to always exhaust W.

In sum, Model B, our revised classical system, is a system in which *relative* quantities of commodities demanded (supplied) depend on the relative prices. Consequently, Model B is rid of the inconsistency of Model A.

This is because as the relative prices change, quantities demanded (supplied) adjust in a relative manner to always exhaust the system's limited flow of resources W.

This reflects how consistency of Model B with limited resources is ensured by the behavior in the system. In contrast, as we have established in Chapter 5.2, consistency of Model A with limited resources is ensured by the non-behavioral Say's Law.

Hence we would expect that Model B is rid of Say's Law since as established, consistency of this system is ensured by the behavior in this system. We shall now confirm in detail that Model B is rid of Say's Law that restricts Model A to long-run states.

6.3 Model B Is Rid Of Say's Law That Restricts Model A to Long-run States

Model B, our revised classical system, appears again below:

Model B

11. $\quad D_j \equiv F_j'\left[W, f(z)\right]$

12. $\quad S_j \equiv G_j'\left[W, g(z)\right]$

13. $\quad E_j'\left[W\{f(z) - g(z)\} = 0\right] = 0$

Let us assume that the overall conditions E_j' [ ] = 0 in (13) vanish the system hence being in general equilibrium. This is only possible if the internal condition $W\{f(z) - g(z)\} = 0$ vanishes.

Next, condition $W\{f(z) - g(z)\} = 0$ can vanish only if the conditions $f(z) - g(z) = 0$ vanish. We shall now examine why conditions $f(z) - g(z) = 0$ of Model B vanish in general equilibrium which will allow us to bring out more fully the nature of the system's equilibrium conditions.

When general equilibrium of the system is established, the quantity of commodities demanded in every market across the system equals the quantity supplied in that market.

This also means that in general equilibrium, the ratios of the quantities of commodities demanded across the system equal the corresponding ratios of the quantities supplied across the system.

Next, functions $f(z)$ determine the $(n - 1)$ ratios of the quantities demanded across the system while functions $g(z)$ determine the $(n - 1)$ ratios of the quantities of commodities supplied across the system.

Hence we may substitute functions $f(z)$ and $g(z)$ into the equilibrium conditions described. This leads to conditions

$f(z)-g(z)=0$ which are $(n-1)$ in number; and the vanishing of these conditions in general equilibrium allows us to solve for the system's $(n-1)$ relative prices.

In sum, Model B automatically meets the counting rule with hence no need to eliminate a surplus equation using Say's Law as has to be done in the case of Model A.

Consequently, Model B is rid of the misused Say's Law that is imposed on Model A and which restricts the system to long-run states. This, as we discussed earlier, is a misused Say's Law because it is not a true identity.

This is because as we established earlier, it is given the substantive role in Model A of ensuring consistency of the system with limited resources. But the Law in being a true identity should not be given such a substantive role.

However, no such substantive role is given to the Law in Model B since it is not required to ensure consistency of the system with limited resources.

Consequently, Model B is rid of the misused Say's Law that characterizes Model A and which restricts the latter system to long-run states.

Yet while Model B is rid of Model A's misused Say's Law that restricts the latter system to long-run states, we shall find that Model B is yet characterized by the Law.

However, as we shall now establish, this is a true identity form of the Law that hence cannot possibly restrict the system to long-run states.

6.4 Further Remarks On Resolving The Issue Of Say's Law

Model B, our revised classical system, appears again below:

Model B

11. $\quad D_j \equiv F_j'\left[W, f(z)\right]$

12. $\quad S_j \equiv G_j'\left[W, g(z)\right]$

13. $\quad E_j'\left[W\{f(z) - g(z)\} = 0\right] = 0$

General equilibrium of Model B prevails when the overall conditions E_j' [ ] $= 0$ in (13) vanish. This, to review, is only possible if the condition $W\{f(z) - g(z)\} = 0$ within (13) simultaneously vanishes.

47

We shall now establish that this latter expression is Model B's internal budget constraint which we referred to in Chapter 2.3.

Functions $f(z)$ in expression $W\{f(z) - g(z)\} = 0$ operate on W to determine relative quantities of commodities demanded. These quantities adjust in a relative manner to always exhaust W, the system's limited resources.

Next, functions $g(z)$ in expression $W\{f(z) - g(z)\} = 0$ operate on W to determine relative quantities of commodities supplied. These quantities adjust in a relative manner to always exhaust W, the system's limited resources.

In sum, expression $W\{f(z) - g(z)\} = 0$ within Model B is the system's budget constraint. However, this is an internal budget constraint in being within the system rather than being imposed on the system from the outside.

Hence this internal budget constraint cannot possibly restrict the system to long-run states. This as we shall now establish gives it the property of being a true identity form of Say's Law.

Let us refer again to expression $W\{f(z) - g(z)\} = 0$ which is Model B's internal budget constraint. To review, functions $f(z)$ in expression $W\{f(z) - g(z)\} = 0$ operate on W to determine relative quantities demanded that adjust in a relative manner to always exhaust W.

Moreover, functions $g(z)$ in $W\{f(z) - g(z)\} = 0$ operate on W to determine relative quantities of commodities supplied that adjust in a relative manner to always exhaust W.

We have focused so far on the variable W as reflecting Model B's limited resources. However, as noted in Chapter 5.2, W also reflects Model B's long-run overall output or income. This meaning of W will now be relevant to our analysis.

When we said that functions $f(z)$ in $W\{f(z) - g(z)\} = 0$ operate on W to determine relative quantities of commodities demanded that exhaust W, we were taking or describing W as the aggregate demand for commodities.

Moreover, when we said that functions $g(z)$ in $W\{f(z) - g(z)\} = 0$ operate on W to determine relative commodities supplied that exhaust W, we were now taking or describing W as the aggregate supply of commodities.

Consequently, Model B is characterized by Say's Law. This is because functions $f(z)$ and $g(z)$ allow us to describe the system's overall output or income W alternately as aggregate demand and aggregate supply.

However, Model B's Say's Law is a true identity form of the Law since as we established, it is solely a descriptive device in the system. We can now confirm our earlier discussion in Chapter 2.3 concerning how we resolve the issue of Say's Law.

To review, Say's Law in Model A is an external budget constraint that is not a true identity and it restricts the system to long-run states. However, Model A's external budget constraint form of Say's Law is transformed into an internal budget constraint in Model B, namely, $W\{f(z)-g(z)\}=0$.

This budget constraint of Model B, in being internal to the system, cannot possibly restrict the system to long-run states. This as we have established, gives this internal budget constraint form of Say's Law the property of being a true identity form of Say's Law.

This confirms that Model B's internal budget constraint form of Say's Law cannot possibly restrict the system to long-run states. In sum, through Model B, we have resolved the longstanding problem brought up by Keynes of Say's Law restricting the orthodox classical system, Model A, to long-run states.

6.5 Additional Comments On Resolving The Issue of Say's Law

Model B, our revised classical system, appears again below:

Model B

11. $\quad D_j \equiv F_j'\left[W, f(z)\right]$

12. $\quad S_j \equiv G_j'\left[W, g(z)\right]$

13. $\quad E_j'\left[W\{f(z)-g(z)\}=0\right]=0$

We have brought additional functions into the overall demand and supply functions of Model B. These are the internal functions, namely, functions $f(z)$ and $g(z)$.

These functions determine only the ratios of the quantities of commodities demanded and the ratios of the quantities of supplied, respectively.

Hence these internal functions in determining only these ratios of quantities cannot, on their own, determine relative quantities of commodities demanded and supplied.

These internal functions of Model B can only determine relative quantities of commodities demanded (supplied) by operating on the system's limited flow of resources W. However, these internal functions are within Model B's overall demand (supply) functions.

As a result, they bring the system's limited resources W from outside the behavioral content of Model A, where it was put by the system's misused Say's Law, into the behavioral content of Model B.

That is, into the demand and supply functions (11) and (12) of Model B. Functions $f(z)$ and $g(z)$ as we have established then operate on W to determine relative quantities of commodities demanded (supplied).

Hence these quantities, in being relative quantities, will each adjust in a relative manner to always sum to the limited resources of Model B. This analysis allows us to see from a further perspective how we have resolved the issue of Say's Law.

The variable W was put outside Model A's behavioral content by Say's Law. However, functions $f(z)$ and $g(z)$ of Model B can only determine relative quantities demanded (supplied) by operating on W.

Next, functions $f(z)$ and $g(z)$ to review are within the behavioral content of Model B. Hence they bring W from outside the behavioral content of Model A into the behavioral content of Model B. This rids Model A of its external budget form of Say's Law that imposes W on the system.

Then W in moving into the behavioral content of Model B, together with functions $f(z)$ and $g(z)$, forms the basis for the system's internal budget constraint form of the Law, namely, $W\{f(z) - g(z)\} = 0$; and we have established that this is a true identity that cannot possibly restrict the system long-run states.

In sum, we have resolved the issue of Say's Law restricting Model A to long-run states in the following way. We first established that Model A is characterized by an external budget constraint form of Say's Law. This is not a true identity and it restricts the system to long-run states.

However, we transformed Model A's external budget constraint form of the Law into an internal budget constraint form of the Law in Model B; and this budget constraint, in being internal to the system, cannot possibly restrict the system to long-run states.

This as we established, gives this budget constraint the property of being a true identity form of Say's Law that hence cannot possibly restrict the latter system to long-run states. Whereas Model A's external budget constraint form of the Law is not a true identity and it restricts the system to long-run states.

6.6 Why Say's Law Became A Problematic Concept In The Literature

Economists rightly insist that price systems must be consistent; and they define consistency of a system to mean that the system must meet the counting rule. That is, the number of independent equations and the number of unknowns must be equal.

This counting rule is imposed on Model A by Say's Law being used to eliminate a surplus equation from the system. However, the Law as Keynes established, restricts the system to long-run states. This book has resolved this quandary in the following way.

Model A in meeting the counting rule is generally taken to mean that the system is consistent. Yet the system reflects the economic inconsistency we have uncovered.

Hence taking consistency of Model A to be ensured solely by imposing Say's Law on the system to eliminate a surplus equation is clearly an unsatisfactory approach to ensuring consistency of the system.

Yet Model A must be subject to this counting rule. This means that we had to find a means other than Say's Law to impose this rule on Model A.

Let us review how this has been accomplished in this book through Model B on account of our uncovering and resolving through Model B, an inconsistency in Model A.

This inconsistency was resolved through Model B by our bringing into this system, an aspect to behavior that ensures consistency of the system with limited resources, an aspect to behavior that is missing from Model A.

This was accomplished by our incorporating functions $f(z)$ and $g(z)$ into Model B's overall demand and supply functions.

Moreover, we established that these functions, and hence the new aspect to behavior that characterizes Model B, also ensure that the system is consistent in the sense of ensuring that the system meets the counting rule.

Hence we ensure consistency of Model B taking consistency of the system to be reflected in the system meeting the counting rule. Clearly, however, Model B meets the counting rule on account of the behavior in the system.

This means that we do not need to ensure that Model B meets the counting rule by imposing Say's Law on the system to eliminate a surplus equation as has to be done in the case of Model A.

This, to review, is because Model B meets the counting rule on account of the behavior in the system. Hence we rid Model B of Model A's misused Say's Law that is imposed on the latter system to eliminate a surplus equation but which restricts Model A to long-run states.

6.7 An Overview Of How Model A's Inconsistency Was Resolved Through Model B

When Model A, the orthodox classical system is written, the system does not initially meet the counting rule. This is because there is a surplus equation in the system over the number of unknowns.

Economists then usually impose Say's Law on the system to eliminate this surplus equation. This ensures that the system meets the counting rule.

However, the Law not only ensures that Model A meets the counting rule. The Law as we established in Chapter 5.2, also simultaneously ensures consistency of the system with limitation in resources.

This brought an economic inconsistency into Model A, since consistency of the system with limitation in resources should be ensured by the behavior in the system rather than by the non-behavioral Say's Law.

We resolved Model A's economic inconsistency through Model B by bringing into the latter system, through the system's functions, an aspect to behavior that ensures consistency of the system with limited resources.

Moreover, as we established in Section 6.3, this accounted for Model B automatically meeting the counting rule. Hence we did not need Say's Law to eliminate a surplus equation from Model B as is the case with Model A.

Consequently, we rid Model B of the misused Say's Law that is required for Model A to meet the counting rule but which restricts the latter system to long-run states. Model A's misused Say's Law was then replaced in Model B with a correctly used Say's Law.

This as we have established in Section 6.4 is a true identity in being simply a descriptive device that hence cannot possibly restrict the system to long-run states or cause other problems commonly attributed to the Law.

6.8 How Model A's Inconsistency Arose And How It Was Resolved Through Model B

Model A's inconsistency arose because the system's functions make *quantities* of commodities demanded (supplied), rather than *relative quantities* of commodities demanded (supplied) depend on the relative prices.

Next, there is a surplus equation in Model A with Say's Law being imposed on the system to eliminate this surplus equation. Hence Model A's functions operate within the confines of Say's Law, with the Law restricting the system to long-run states. Let us review how this has been resolved through Model B.

Model B makes *relative* quantities of commodities demanded (supplied) depend on the relative prices. Moreover, this accounts for Model B automatically meeting the counting rule as we confirmed in Section 6.3.

Hence we do not need Say's Law to eliminate a surplus equation from Model B. Consequently, Model B's functions are not confined within a misused Say's Law as is the case with Model A's functions.

This explains why Model B is not restricted by the Law to long-run states, a reflection of the system having a more general character than Model A which is restricted by a misused Say's Law to long-run states.

6.9 Summary

We developed our new type of demand and supply functions in detail in this chapter. These functions then provided the basis for our revised classical system, Model B.

53

This is a system in which *relative* quantities of commodities demanded (supplied) depend on the relative commodity prices. This accounted for Model B being rid of the inconsistency of Model A.

This is because the quantities of commodities demanded and supplied in Model B, in being relative quantities, adjust in a relative manner as the relative prices change to always exhaust the system's limited resources.

Consequently, the behavior in Model B ensures consistency of the system with limited resources. This accounts for Model B being rid of the inconsistency of Model A.

This inconsistency, to review, arose because consistency of the latter system is ensured by Say's Law rather than by the behavior in the system. Moreover, Model A is restricted by Say's Law to long-run states.

However, we established that Model B, in being rid of the inconsistency of Model A, is characterized by a correctly used Say's Law. This as we established in Section 6.4 is a true identity in being simply a descriptive device hence it cannot possibly restrict the system to long-run states.

Chapter 7

Resolving The Price Level Indeterminacy Of The Neoclassical System

7.1 Introduction

Patinkin as we discussed in Chapter 3.6 has held that Model A, which we shall also now take to represent the neoclassical system, is characterized by an indeterminate price level and an invalid dichotomy between its real and monetary sectors. However, we shall establish in this chapter that Model B is rid of these problems.

7.2 Review Of Model A's Price Level Indeterminacy

Model A, the orthodox classical system, appears below:

Model A

$$4. \qquad D_j \equiv F_j \left[z \right]$$

$$5. \qquad S_j \equiv G_j \left[z \right]$$

$$6. \qquad E_j \left[z \right] = 0$$

As in Chapter 3.6, we impose the following long-run Cambridge cash-balance equation on the system:

$$8. \qquad K \left[p_1 X_1 + p_2 X_2 + \cdots p_n X_n \right] = M$$

The variable K represents the proportion of their money income that individuals and firms hold as a cash balance. We also assume that these balances are held only for transactions purposes. That is, to offset any possible lack of synchronization between payments and receipts.

We also show Walras Law below this being Model A's budget constraint:

14. $$D + (M_d - M_s) - S = 0$$

D and S represent the aggregate demand and the aggregate supply of commodities both of these variables being measured in money. While M_d and M_s denote the demand and supply of money to hold respectively.

Walras Law implies that any excess demand (supply) of money is accompanied by an equal excess supply (demand) for commodities.

Let us, however, move the price level of Model A from equilibrium by making an equiproportionate change in the individual money prices. This, referring to the cash-balance equation (8), creates an excess demand (supply) of money to hold.

However, the commodity markets remain in equilibrium since they depend on the relative prices that remain in unchanged when the price level is moved from equilibrium.

That is, no commodity market comes out of equilibrium to move the price level back to equilibrium. Hence Model A's price level is indeterminate.

Clearly also, Walras Law is violated in the system since referring to expression (14), an excess supply (demand) for commodities does not appear when the price level is moved from equilibrium.

This is because, as we noted, the commodity markets remain in equilibrium when the price level is moved from equilibrium. This is because they depend on the relative prices which remain unchanged when the price level is moved from equilibrium.

Patinkin approached Model A's price level indeterminacy by incorporating a real balance variable into his system which accounts for his system's price level being determinate.

However, the real balance effect operates only when Patinkin's system is out of long-run equilibrium and falls out of his system in long-run equilibrium. Hence we return to the long-run Model A that is characterized by an indeterminate price level.

We shall now establish that the price level of our revised classical system, Model B, is determinate with the system hence also being rid of Model A's invalid real-monetary dichotomy.

7.3 Model B's Price Level Is Determinate

Model B, our revised classical system, appears again below:

Model B

11. $\quad D_j \equiv F_j'\left[W, f(z)\right]$

12. $\quad S_j \equiv G_j'\left[W, g(z)\right]$

13. $\quad E_j'\left[W\{f(z) - g(z)\} = 0\right] = 0$

The Cambridge cash balance equation also appears again below:

8. $\qquad K\left[p_1 X_1 + p_2 X_2 + \cdots p_n X_n\right] = M$

Walras Law which is Model B's budget constraint, is also shown again below:

14. $\qquad D + (M_d - M_s) - S = 0$

Let us hold the relative commodity prices fixed throughout Model B and move the price level from equilibrium. This, to review, is through our making an equiproportionate change in every individual money price in (8).

This throws equation (8) out of equilibrium to hence show some excess demand (supply) of money to hold. Next, Walras Law should show in an equal excess supply (demand) for commodities.

Moreover, Model B commodity markets in the aggregate do come out of equilibrium to show an equal excess supply (demand) for commodities. Consequently, a market process is set up to move the system's price level to equilibrium, Model B's price level hence being determinate.

Let us now establish why Model B's commodity markets in the aggregate can come out of equilibrium when the price level is moved from equilibrium, since this is a key property of Model B that distinguishes the system from Model A.

While Model A's functions determine n quantities of commodities demanded (supplied) as functions of the relative prices, Model B's functions determine $(n-1)$ *relative* commodity demands (supplies) as functions of the relative prices.

This explains why when there is an excess demand (supply) of money, Model B's budget constraint, which is Walras

Law, shows that there is an equal excess supply (demand) for commodities.

This is because the existence of this overall excess supply (demand) for commodities in Model B is perfectly consistent with the *relative* commodity demands (supplies) that are determined in the real part of the system.

Consequently, there are market forces in Model B to move the system back to equilibrium since Walras Law holds when the system is out of equilibrium.

Yet Model B is a dichotomized system because we solve for the relative commodity prices, the z, from conditions $f(z)-g(z)=0$ of Model B without specifying the price level. Clearly, however, this is a valid dichotomy since it does not cause the system's price level to be indeterminate.

Model A is also characterized by a dichotomy since we also solve for the relative prices in the system without specifying the price level. However, Model A's dichotomy as Patinkin has emphasized is invalid, since it accounts for the system's price level being indeterminate.

7.4 Why Model A's Price Level Indeterminacy Could Be Resolved

Model A, the orthodox classical system appears below:

Model A

4. $\quad D_j = F_j[z]$

5. $\quad S_j = G_j[z]$

6. $\quad E_j[z]=0$

Functions (4) and (5) make absolute commodity demands and supplies depend on the relative prices. Hence these absolute commodity demands (supplies) are determined independently of the monetary sector.

This explains why Model A's price level is indeterminate; since were the price level moved from equilibrium, the commodity markets remain in equilibrium.

This is because absolute commodity demands (supplies) depend on the relative prices which remain unchanged when the price level is moved from equilibrium. Hence no market equilibrating process is set up to move the price level back to equilibrium with the price level hence being indeterminate.

Clearly, Model A's price level is indeterminate because absolute quantities of commodities demanded (supplied) in depending on the relative prices, remain unchanged when the price level is moved from equilibrium.

Hence no market equilibrating process is set up to move the price level back to equilibrium, the price level hence being indeterminate.

However, only *relative* commodity demands and *relative* commodity supplies can be determined independently of the monetary sector of the classical system. Let us go into this in detail through focusing on Model B, our revised classical system, which appears again below:

Model B

11. $\quad D_j \equiv F_j'\left[W, f(z)\right]$

12. $\quad S_j \equiv G_j'\left[W, g(z)\right]$

13. $\quad E_j'\left[W\{f(z) - g(z)\} = 0\right] = 0$

We solve for Model B's relative prices, the z, from conditions $f(z) - g(z) = 0$ independently of the system's price level. These conditions stem from functions (11) and (12) that make *relative* commodity demands (supplies) depend on the relative prices, the z.

Consequently, it is these *relative* commodity demands (supplies) that are independent of the monetary sector of Model B. This accounts for us resolving through Model B the price level indeterminacy of Model A along the lines that we have discussed.

Clearly, the key difference between Model A and Model B is as follows: the real sector of Model B determines $(n-1)$ *relative* commodity demands (supplies) as functions of the relative prices. Hence Walras Law can operate in Model B when the system is out of equilibrium.

On the other hand, the real sector of Model A determines *absolute* commodity demands (supplies) as functions of the relative prices for all n commodities. This explains why Walras Law cannot possibly hold in Model A when the system is out of equilibrium.

7.5 Further Remarks on Resolving Model A's Price Level Indeterminacy and Invalid Dichotomy

We show Model B, our revised classical system again below:

Model B

11. $\quad D_j \equiv F_j'\left[W, f(z)\right]$

12. $\quad S_j \equiv G_j'\left[W, g(z)\right]$

13. $\quad E_j'\left[W\{f(z) - g(z)\} = 0\right] = 0$

We have rid Model B of Model A's inconsistency by bringing an aspect to behavior into Model B that ensures consistency of the system with limited resources. This was accomplished by our incorporating functions $f(z)$ and $g(z)$ into Model B's demand and supply functions.

Next, we have established that on account of these functions, we have rid Model B of Model A's price level indeterminacy and related invalid dichotomy. We may also put this analysis in the following way.

Had we not resolved Model A's inconsistency through Model B, the microeconomic conditions of this latter system, namely, conditions $f(z)-g(z)=0$ in (13) would have to be replaced by those of the orthodox Model A that were set out in Chapter 3.4. That is, by the latter system's excess-demand equations $E_j[z]=0$ of Model A.

When we solve the latter conditions for the relative prices, this implies general equilibrium. That is, every commodity market is cleared. Hence there is no role for the price level which remains indeterminate.

However, in ridding Model A of inconsistency through Model B, we replaced the set of orthodox microeconomic conditions $E_j[z]=0$ of Model A with the set of microeconomic conditions $f(z)-g(z)=0$ in (13) of Model B. This system, as we discussed in detail in Sections 7.3 and 7.4, is rid of the price level indeterminacy and invalid real-monetary dichotomy of Model A.

Finally, Lange prior to Patinkin had brought out a contradiction in Model A which Lange took as a classical system. Lange formed Model A by imposing Say's Law on the system then he deduced the "homogeneity postulate" from the Law.

Next, Lange held that while Say's Law is imposed on Model A in order to ensure money neutrality, the Law accounts for the system's price level being indeterminate. This led Lange to conclude that there is a contradiction in Model A.[9]

This is because if the system's price level is to be made determinate, money neutrality must be abandoned through Say's Law being removed from the system. However, this contradiction in Model A that Lange pointed to has also been resolved through Model B.

This is because money is neutral in Model B since we solve for the system's relative prices independently of the price level. Moreover, the system's price level as we have established is determinate. This reflects how we have rid Model B of the contradiction in Model A that Lange brought out.

7.6 Summary

Patinkin has held that Model A, which we also take to represent the neoclassical system, is characterized by an indeterminate price level and an invalid dichotomy between its real and monetary sectors.

However, we established that these problems with Model A stem from the inconsistency we have uncovered in the system. Hence in resolving this inconsistency through Model B, we rid the latter system of the problems of Model A brought out by Patinkin.

Clearly, the key difference between Model A and Model B is that the real sector of the latter system determines $(n-1)$ *relative* commodity demands (supplies) as functions of the relative prices. On the other hand, the real sector of Model A determines *absolute* commodity demands (supplies) for all n commodities.

This difference between the systems means that Walras Law can operate in Model B when the system is out of equilibrium. This, however, is impossible in the case of Model A. This accounts for the latter system being characterized by an indeterminate price level and an invalid real-monetary dichotomy.

---

[9] O. Lange, "Say's Law: A Restatement and Criticism," in *Studies in Mathematical Economics and Econometrics* (Chicago, *1942*), pps. 49-68.

Next, Model B is a dichotomized system in that we can solve for the system's relative prices without specifying the price level. However, Model B's dichotomy is not invalid unlike Model A's dichotomy.

This is because Model B's dichotomy does not cause the system's price level to be indeterminate. Whereas Model A's dichotomy is invalid in accounting for the system's price level indeterminacy.

Chapter 8

Generality Of The New Approach To Price Systems

8.1 Introduction

We have through Model B, our revised classical system, arrived at a very general approach to price systems. This is a result of Model B being rid of an inconsistency in the orthodox classical system, Model A.

This inconsistency arose because Model A lacks an aspect to behavior that should ensure consistency of the system with limited resources. This accounts for Model A being restricted to long-run states by a misused Say's Law.

However, we resolved Model A's inconsistency through Model B by bringing into the latter system the aspect to behavior that is missing from Model A. We then established in Chapter 6 that Model B, unlike Model A, is not restricted by Say's long-run states.

Moreover, we established in the preceding chapter that Model B is also rid of the price level indeterminacy and invalid real-monetary dichotomy of Model A, problems brought out by Patinkin.

8.2 Contrasting The General Economic Rationale Of Model A And Model B

Model A and Model B are both characterized by the identical variable W that reflects the systems' limited flow of resources. Model A and Model B also both reflect consistency with limitation in resources, the systems hence reflecting the *general logic* of price systems.

Now Model A's functions determine *absolute* quantities of commodities demanded (supplied) as functions of the relative prices. However, as illustrated by Model B, we should make *relative* quantities of commodities depend on the relative prices.

This accounts for Model B reflecting not simply the *general logic* of price systems but also the *general economic logic* of price systems. This is because consistency of the system with limited resources is ensured by the behavior in the system.

Next, Model A is found to be characterized by a surplus equation over the number of unknowns. Economists then impose Say's Law on the system to eliminate this surplus equation to ensure consistency of the system.

Say's Law as discussed in Chapter 5.2, then ensures consistency of the system with limited resources. However, this brings inconsistency into Model A.

This is because consistency of the system with limited resources should be ensured by the behavior in the system rather than by Say's Law. We may put this analysis in the following way.

Model A does reflect consistency with limited resources, the system hence reflecting the *general logic* of price systems. However, Model A does not reflect the *general economic logic* of price systems. This is because consistency of the system is not ensured by the behavior in the system but is ensured by Say's Law.

Turning now to Model B, we find that this system's demand and supply functions determine relative quantities of commodities demanded (supplied) as functions of the relative prices.

Hence quantities demanded (supplied) in Model B, in being relative quantities, adjust in a relative manner to always sum to W. This ensures that Model B reflects consistency with limited resources.

Consequently, consistency of Model B with limited resources is ensured by the behavior in the system, the system hence reflecting the *general economic logic* of price systems. This accounts for Model B being rid of the inconsistency of Model A.   .

This, to review, is because Model A's inconsistency stems from consistency of the system with limited resources being ensured by the non-behavioral Say's Law rather than by the behavior in the system.

8.3 Resolving The Problems With Model A Brought Out By Keynes And Patinkin

Price systems, in general should not be restricted to particular states. Moreover, the systems should be characterized by a determinate price level. That is, the systems should be able to deal with issues concerning the stability of monetary equilibrium.

Keynes, however, held that Model A is restricted to long-run states by Say's Law while Patinkin held that Model A's price level is indeterminate with the system being subject to an invalid real-monetary dichotomy.

These criticisms of Model A by Keynes and Patinkin led to a substantial literature concerning Say's Law and the issue of Model A's price level indeterminacy and invalid real-monetary dichotomy.

However, this literature focused on *symptoms* or consequences of the inconsistency we have uncovered in Model A rather than on this inconsistency itself. This is because as we have established, this inconsistency is the cause of the problems with Model A that were brought out by Keynes and Patinkin.

Hence in resolving this inconsistency through Model B, we satisfactorily rid this system of the problems with the orthodox classical system, Model A, that were brought out by Keynes and Patinkin.

That is, as discussed in Chapter 6, we rid Model B of Model A's misused Say's Law that restricts the latter system to long-run states. As well in Chapter 7, we rid Model B of Model A's price level indeterminacy and invalid real-monetary dichotomy,

8.4 Model B Is Wholly Behavioral In Character

We have already established that Model B is wholly behavioral in character. This is because the system is rid of the misused Say's Law that restricts Model A to long-run states. This was then replaced in Model B with a true identity form of the Law.

This is simply a descriptive device hence it cannot possibly influence the behavioral character of the system, indicating that the system is wholly behavioral in character. However, we shall find it useful to confirm that Model B is wholly behavioral in character.

There are a number of properties that are needed to form consistent price systems and we shall focus on two of these that are of particular relevance to the analyses of this book.

We shall then show that these two properties are ensured in Model B by the behavior in the system. This is as would be expected since as we have established, Model B reflects the *general economic logic* of price systems.

On the other hand, we shall find that the two properties we consider that are needed to form consistent price systems are ensured in Model A by the system's misused Say's Law.

This is also as would be expected since Model A, while reflecting the *general logic* of price systems, does not reflect the *general economic logic* of the systems. This is because consistency of the system with limited resources is ensured by Say's Law rather than by the behavior in the system.

The two general requirements for a consistent price system that we shall consider are first, that the system should reflect the general economic logic of price systems. Second, the system must solve for equilibrium quantities and prices.

We shall now establish that these two conditions are brought into Model B by the behavior in the system. Model B appears again below:

Model B

11. $\quad D_j \equiv F'_j\left[W, f(z)\right]$

12. $\quad S_j \equiv G'_j\left[W, g(z)\right]$

13. $\quad E'_j\left[W\{f(z) - g(z)\} = 0\right] = 0$

We have already established that Model B reflects the general economic logic of price systems since consistency of the system with limited resources is ensured by the behavior in the system. This is a new condition for consistency of price systems that is introduced in this book.

Next, when Model B is in general equilibrium, the overall conditions E'_j [ ] = 0 in (13) vanish. This requires that the term $W\{f(z) - g(z)\} = 0$ that is within equations (13) simultaneously vanish. This occurs on account of conditions $f(z) - g(z) = 0$ vanishing in general equilibrium.

Moreover, conditions $f(z) - g(z) = 0$ as we have established are $(n-1)$ in number hence they are just equal to the number of variables to be determined which are the $(n-1)$ relative prices. Hence Model B automatically meets the counting rule.

This means that the system's equilibrium quantities and prices are determined; and this is due to the new aspect to behavior that we brought into the system through functions $f(z)$ and $g(z)$.

In sum, the behavior in Model B brings into the system the two properties to which we referred that are required to form a consistent price system.

More precisely, it is the new aspect to behavior that we brought into Model B, through functions $f(z)$ and $g(z)$, that brings these two properties into Model B. Model A, in contrast, lacks the new aspect to behavior that we brought into Model B through functions $f(z)$ and $g(z)$.

This, as we shall now discuss, accounts for the two general properties we consider that are required to form a consistent price system being brought into Model A by the non-behavioral Say's Law rather than by the behavior in the system.

8.5 Model A Is Not Wholly Behavioral In Character

We have established in Chapter 5.2 that Model A is made consistent with limitation in resources by a misused Say's Law being imposed on the system to eliminate a surplus equation.

That is, the system's general logic, as reflected in consistency of the system with limitation in resources, stems from the system's Say's Law.

Hence while Model A reflects the *general logic* of price systems in reflecting consistency with limited resources, the system does not reflect the *general economic logic* of price systems. This is because consistency of the system with limited resources is not ensured by the behavior in the system.

Next, we have established that Model A meets the counting rule on account of Say's Law being used eliminate a surplus equation from the system. That is, Say's Law rather than the behavior in the system allows us to solve for the system's equilibrium quantities and prices.

In sum, the two general properties we considered that are required for a consistent price system are brought into Model A by the non-behavioral Say's Law. This confirms that Model A is not wholly behavioral in character.

In contrast, as discussed in the preceding section, the two general requirements for a consistent price system that we have listed are brought into Model B by the behavior in the system rather than by Say's Law. This confirmed that Model B is wholly behavioral in character.

8.6 Deriving Model A From Model B

We shall now establish that we may derive Model A from Model B. This will allow us to confirm that Model B has a more general character than Model A.

We proceed by first showing Model A, the orthodox classical system below:

Model A

4. $D_j \equiv F_j[z]$

5. $S_j \equiv G_j[z]$

6. $E_j[z] = 0$

Next, Model B, our revised classical system appears below:

Model B

11. $D_j \equiv F_j'\big[W, f(z)\big]$

12. $S_j \equiv G_j'\big[W, g(z)\big]$

13. $E_j'\big[W\{f(z) - g(z)\} = 0\big] = 0$

The relative prices, the z, influence the commodity demands and supplies in both Model A and Model B. However, unlike Model A, the relative prices in Model B influence these demands and supplies through the system's internal functions, namely, functions $f(z)$ and $g(z)$.

Moreover, it is through these internal functions that we brought the aspect to behavior that ensures consistency of Model B with limited resources. We thereby brought the *general economic logic* that should characterize all price systems, into Model B.

Let us now remove these internal functions from the demand and supply functions of Model B while leaving the z as independent variables in these latter functions.

Functions $f(z)$ and $g(z)$ as we discussed in Chapter 6.5, had brought the variable W from outside the behavioral content of Model A into the demand and supply functions of Model B.

Hence W is also removed from the demand and supply functions of Model B with the removal of functions $f(z)$ and $g(z)$. Consequently, we transform Model B into Model A.

However, as we discussed earlier, Model A into which we have transformed Model B, is inconsistent in an economic sense; and this also accounts for Model A being inconsistent in the sense of not meeting the counting rule since there is a surplus equation over the number of unknowns in the system.

Let us now follow the orthodox literature and impose Say's Law on Model A to eliminate this surplus equation. However, we have established that this is a misused form of the Law.

This misused Say's Law as we discussed in Chapter 5.2, then imposes on Model A the variable W that has been removed from within the behavioral content of Model B. That is, W is now put outside the behavioral content of Model A where it forms the basis for an external budget constraint.

Individual quantities of commodities demanded and supplied then emerge from this budget constraint. This ensures that Model A is consistent with limitation in resources.

Such consistency, however, is ensured by the system's misused Say's Law rather than by the behavior in the system. This, of course, is the inconsistency that we have uncovered in Model A.

This inconsistency, however, has been resolved through Model B on account of the new aspect to behavior that we have brought into the system.

This is because this new aspect to behavior as we have established, ensures consistency of Model B with limitation in resources. Hence through Model B we resolved Model A's economic inconsistency.

This is because Model A's inconsistency stems from consistency of the system with limitation in resources being ensured by Say's Law rather than by the behavior in the system

In sum, we have established that we may derive Model A from Model B. This confirms that Model B has a more general character than Model A.

This is because deriving Model B from Model A required restricting the generality of Model B. This is by removing from the latter system the new aspect to behavior that we incorporated into the system through functions $f(z)$ and $g(z)$.

8.7 Model A's Inconsistency Arises Within The System's Behavioral Content

Model A's inconsistency is economic in character since it arises because an aspect to behavior that should ensure consistency of the system with limited resource is missing from the system.

Hence to resolve this inconsistency, we needed to adapt the system's demand (supply) functions to bring this missing aspect to behavior into the system.

Let us review how this was accomplished through Model B which appears again below:

Model B

11. $\quad D_j \equiv F_j'\big[W, f(z)\big]$

12. $\quad S_j \equiv G_j'\big[W, g(z)\big]$

13. $\quad E_j'\big[W\{f(z) - g(z)\} = 0\big] = 0$

We brought the aspect to behavior that ensures consistency of Model B with limited resources by bringing functions $f(z)$ and $g(z)$ into the system's demand and supply functions.

These latter functions operate on W, the system's limited resources, to determine relative quantities of commodities demanded (supplied). These quantities demanded (supplied) then adjust in a relative manner as the relative prices change to always exhaust the system's limited resources W.

In sum, consistency of Model B with limited resources is ensured by the behavior in the system rather than by Say's Law as in Model A. Consequently, Model B is rid of the inconsistency in the behavioral content of Model A.

This was accomplished by our bringing into Model B an aspect to behavior that ensures consistency of the system with limited resources, an aspect to behavior that is missing from Model A.

This accounted for Model B having a more general character than Model A which is reflected in various ways. Model B, for example, is characterized by the internal budget constraint $W\{f(z) - g(z)\} = 0$ that is within equations (13) of the system.

This as we established in Chapter 6.4 is a budget constraint that reflects a true identity form of Say's Law hence it cannot possibly restrict the system to long-run states. Whereas Model A's misused Say's Law is an external budget constraint that is not a true identity and which restricts the system to long-run states.

8.8 Summary

We have set out our revised classical system, Model B, in Chapter 6 and through this system, we resolved the inconsistency we have uncovered in Model A, the orthodox classical system. This inconsistency arose because Model A lacks an aspect to behavior that should ensure consistency of the system with limited resources.

However, we brought this aspect to behavior into Model B through functions $f(z)$ and $g(z)$ to rid the system of Model A's inconsistency. We then confirmed that Model B, unlike Model A, is wholly behavioral in character

We also established that we may derive Model A from Model B. This allowed us to confirm that Model B has a more general character than Model A.

This is because reducing Model B to Model A requires restricting the generality of Model B. This is through removing from Model B functions $f(z)$ and $g(z)$ that reflect the new aspect to behavior that we brought into the system.

Chapter 9

Say's Law And The Classical And Keynesian Systems

9.1 Introduction

Keynes held in the *General Theory* that Model A, the orthodox classical system, is restricted by Say's Law to long-run states. However, we established that while Model A is restricted to long-run states by the Law, this is because of a misused form of Say's Law that characterizes the system.

This misused Say's Law enters Model A because of the inconsistency we uncovered in the system. Hence to resolve the problem of Model A being restricted to long-run states by the system's misused Say's Law, we needed to rid the system of its inconsistency.

This was accomplished through Model B, our revised classical system, hence this system is rid of Model A's misused Say's Law. Moreover, this is accomplished in a manner that ensures that Model B is wholly microeconomic in character.

Keynes also rid his system of Model A's misused form of Say's Law; and in this chapter we shall go further into how this is ensured in a manner that accounts for the microeconomics of the Keynesian system being largely suppressed.

9.2 Remarks On Say's Law

Few concepts in economics have caused such problems as Say's Law, the "Law" that "supply creates its own demand."[10] We are referring to the identity form of the Law that appears in or is implied in various classical writings.

Keynes and many other economists impute this identity form of Say's Law to the classical system. This form of the Law, as discussed in Chapter 3.5, is represented by an identity between the aggregate demand and aggregate supply of commodities.

---

[10] On Say's Law see J.B. Say, *A Treatise on Political Economy*, trans. by C.R. Prinsep (1834), pps. 138-39.

Becker and Baumol have referred to this identity form of the Law as Say's Identity.[11] However, we shall retain the term Say's Law to describe this identity since it is better known in the literature.

Keynes held that Say's Law is the "axiom of parallels" of the classical system. That is, according to Keynes, given the Law, all the other basic properties of the classical system follow. Hence the Law, to Keynes, was what accounted for the classical system, which we represent by Model A, being restricted to long-run states.[12]

Economists have also shown that Say's Law gives rise to other problems with Model A. This is through the Law preventing money and market processes from being integrated into Model A in a consistent manner. This, in turn, as Patinkin held, invalidly dichotomizes the system into real and monetary parts.[13]

In fact, so problematic has Say's Law become that some economists have attempted to interpret the Law in alternative ways that imply that it is not a part of the classical system or that it is not an identity.

This has led to a conflicting literature on the Law. Patinkin, for example, in his *Money, Interest, And Prices,* held that Say's Law is not a basic part of the classical system.

Yet Patinkin also recognized that there is evidence that supports the contrary view that the Law is indeed a part of the system.[14] Other conflicting views also characterize parts of the substantial literature on the Law, a literature we cannot cover in any detail here.[15]

However, attempts to interpret Say's Law to show that it is not an identity or that it is not a part of the classical system cannot satisfactorily resolve the issue of the Law. This is because we show in this book that the Law is, indeed, an identity or truism in our revised classical system, Model B.

This means that when properly interpreted, it can have no substantive role in the latter system. However, Say's Law as

---

[11] G.S. Becker and W.J. Baumol, "The Classical Monetary Theory: The Outcome of the Discussion," *Economica,* XIX (1952), pps. 356-7.

[12] Keynes, *op. cit.,* Ch. 2.

[13] See Keynes, *op.cit.,* Ch. 3, Lange, *op. cit. (1942),* pps. 49-68 and Patinkin, *op.cit.,* Ch.VIII.

[14] Patinkin, *op. cit.,* pps.193 and 645. See also Becker and Baumol, *op. cit.,* pps. 371-75 for a discussion that reflects how unclear is the literature on Say's Law.

[15] For summaries of parts of this literature see, for example, Patinkin, *op. cit.,* pps. 645-50 and Becker and Baumol, *op. cit.,* pps. 355-76.

we establish in this book became a problematic concept in the literature because the Law is misused in the orthodox classical system, Model A. This is due to the inconsistency that we have uncovered in the system which led to substantive roles being attributed to the Law in the system.

For example, the Law in Model A, as we discussed in Chapter 5.2, is given the role of ensuring consistency of the system with limited resources. However, the Law in being a true identity should not be given such a substantive role.

Hence the Law in Model A in being given the substantive role described, is clearly an incorrect or misused Say's Law; and it is this incorrect or misused Say's Law that restricts Model A to long-run states.

However, in resolving Model A's inconsistency through Model B, we rid the Law in the latter system of the substantive role we described that is attributed to the Law in Model A. This accounts for a correct Say's Law entering Model B.

This, as we confirmed in Chapter 6.4, is a form of the Law that is a true identity that hence cannot possibly restrict the system to long-run states.

9.3 Say's Law And The New Aspect To Behavior Of Model B

Model B, our revised classical system, appears again below:

$$\textbf{Model B}$$

11. $\quad D_j \equiv F'_j\left[W, f(z)\right]$

12. $\quad S_j \equiv G'_j\left[W, g(z)\right]$

13. $\quad E'_j\left[W\{f(z) - g(z)\} = 0\right] = 0$

Model B as we discussed earlier, reflects the *general economic logic* that should underlie all price systems. This is because the system is characterized by an aspect to behavior that ensures consistency of the system with limited resources, an aspect to behavior that is missing from Model A.

However, as we shall now establish, this new aspect to behavior could characterize Model B only because the system is rid of Model A's incorrect or misused Say's Law that restricts the latter system to long-run states.

We discussed in Chapter 6.3 how within Model B's demand and supply functions of Model B are the internal functions $f(z)$ and $g(z)$. These functions determine only the ratios of the quantities of commodities demanded (supplied).

Hence these internal or interior functions, on their own, cannot determine relative quantities of commodities demanded (supplied). These interior functions of Model B can only determine relative quantities of commodities demanded (supplied) by operating on the system's limited flow of resources W.

However, these interior functions are within Model B's overall demand (supply) functions. As a result, they bring the system's limited flow of resources W into the behavioral content of Model B. Let us review how this rids Model B of Model A's incorrect or misused Say's Law.

The variable W reflects the limited flow of resources of both Model A and Model B. However, Model A's misused Say's Law puts W outside the system's behavioral content.

This accounted for Model A being characterized by an external budget constraint. This is a misused Say's Law in not being a true identity; and it restricts the system to long-run states.

However, the internal functions of Model B bring W from outside the behavioral content of Model A into the behavioral content of Model B.

Hence since Model A's misused Say's Law had put W outside the system's behavioral content, we rid Model B of this misused Say's Law of Model A. This as we established in Chapter 6.3 accounted for Model B automatically meeting the counting rule.

Consequently, we did not need Model A's misused Say's Law to ensure consistency of Model B by eliminating a surplus equation as has to be done in the case of Model A. This accounts for Model B being rid of Model A's misused Say's Law that is imposed on the system to eliminate a surplus equation.

Model A's misused Say's Law, to review, is an external budget constraint that is not a true identity which explains why it restricts the system to long-run states.

However, this external budget constraint of Model A is transformed into an internal budget constraint in Model B. This budget constraint in being internal to the system cannot possibly restrict the system to long-run states.

This as we discussed in Chapter 6.4, gives Model B's internal budget constraint the property of being a true identity form of the Law which explains why it cannot possibly restrict this system to long-run states.

Moreover, individual quantities of commodities emerge from Model B's internal budget constraint which ensures that the system is wholly microeconomic in character.

In sum, we rid Model B of Model A's misused Say's Law that restricts the latter system to long-run states while ensuring that Model B is wholly microeconomic in character.

Whereas Keynes as we discussed earlier, rid his system of Model A misused Say's Law in a manner that suppresses the microeconomics of parts of his system.

These are the parts of the Keynesian system that are based on Keynes' aggregate demand and supply functions. We shall now go further into this finding concerning the Keynesian system.

9.4 Alternative Approaches To Model A's Misused Say's Law

We discussed how we have rid Model B of Model A's misused Say's Law; and we shall find it useful to contrast this in detail with how Keynes rid his system of this misused Say's Law.

This misused Say's Law enters Model A because the system's approach to microeconomics is restricted in generality. This is because Model A lacks an aspect to behavior that should ensure consistency of the system with limited resources.

This means that there are two ways in which we may rid Model A of the system's misused Say's Law. We may generalize the microeconomics of Model A by incorporating into the system an aspect to behavior that ensures consistency of the system with limited resources.

This is the approach to Model A that we followed in this book through Model B. This was accomplished by our bringing into Model B, an aspect to behavior that ensures consistency of the system with limited resources.

This accounted for us ridding Model B of Model A's misused Say's Law while ensuring that Model B is wholly microeconomic in character. Keynes, in contrast, followed a different approach to ridding his system of Model A's misused Say's Law.

This was through Keynes resorting to macroeconomic analysis as reflected in his use of aggregate demand and supply functions. These functions, however, suppress the microeconomics of the parts of the Keynesian system that are based on these functions.

Now our approach to ridding Model B of Model A's misused Say's Law was possible only because through Model B we resolved the inconsistency of Model A.

This inconsistency was resolved on account of our bringing into Model B, an aspect to behavior that ensures consistency of the system with limited resources.

This new aspect to behavior as we have established, provided the basis for us to rid Model B of Model A's misused Say's Law in a satisfactory manner. That is, to rid Model B of Model A's misused Say's Law while ensuring that Model B is wholly microeconomic in character.

9.5 Further Remarks On Model A's Misused Say's Law

We rid Model B of the inconsistency of Model A by bringing into Model B an aspect to behavior that ensures consistency of the system with limited resources, an aspect to behavior that is missing from Model A.

We thereby gave Model B a more general microeconomic character compared to Model A. Moreover, Model B was also thereby simultaneously rid of Model A's misused Say's Law that restricts this system to long-run states.

Consequently, Model B is wholly microeconomic in character but the system is not restricted to long-run states by Model A's misused Say's Law.

Keynes, in contrast, removed Model A's misused Say's Law from his system by wholly suppressing in his system Model A's microeconomic demand and supply functions, functions that give rise to the system's inconsistency. This was accomplished through Keynes forming aggregate demand and supply functions.

These functions allow the aggregate demand and supply of commodities in Keynes' system to diverge which rids his system of Model A's misused Say's Law. However, these functions suppress the microeconomics of the parts of the Keynesian system that is based on these functions.

In sum, Keynes rid his system of Model A's misused Say's Law through macroeconomic analysis. This means that the Keynesian system is not restricted to long-run states by Model A's misused Say's Law. However, as we have discussed, the microeconomics of the Keynesian system is largely suppressed.

Chapter 9

9.6 Remarks On The Classical And Keynesian Systems

We show Model B, our revised classical system, again below:

Model B

11. $\quad D_j \equiv F_j'\left[W, f(z)\right]$

12. $\quad S_j \equiv G_j'\left[W, g(z)\right]$

13. $\quad E_j'\left[W\{f(z) - g(z)\} = 0\right] = 0$

General equilibrium of Model B prevails when the overall condition E_j' [ ] = 0 in (13) vanishes. This is only possible were the condition $W\{f(z) - g(z)\} = 0$ to simultaneously vanish.

This expression that is within equations (13) is, to review, the internal budget constraint of Model B which replaces Model A's external budget constraint form of Say's Law.

Now the variable W as we discussed in Chapter 6.3, is brought into Model B by functions $f(z)$ and $g(z)$, functions that bring into Model B an aspect to behavior that ensures consistency of the system with limited resources,

These functions lead to conditions $f(z)-g(z)\neq0$ which with W give rise to the system's internal budget constraint. Namely, expression $W\{f(z) - g(z)\} = 0$.

On the other hand, Model A lacks the aspect to behavior described in lacking functions $f(z)$ and $g(z)$ and condition $f(z)-g(z)\neq0$. Hence W could not possibly be brought into the behavioral content of Model A.

This results in W being put outside the behavioral content of Model A where it forms the basis for the system's external budget constraint.

This external budget constraint of Model A as discussed earlier, is not a true identity form of Say's Law and it restricts the system to long-run states. However, there is another property of Model A's misused Say's Law to be considered.

Although Say's Law is misused in Model A it yet forms the basis in the system for a budget constraint of relevance to microeconomics.

This is because individual quantities of commodities demanded (supplied) emerge from this budget constraint which reflects how the system is microeconomic in character. Let us go further into this issue.

9.7 Further Comments On The Classical And Keynesian Systems

We have established that we have rid Model B of Model A's misused Say's Law by incorporating into Model B, an aspect to behavior that ensures consistency of the system with limited resources

However, this new aspect to behavior of Model B rids this system *only* of the property of Model A's incorrect Say's Law that restricts the system to long-run states.

This, of course, explains why through Model B we resolved the issue of Model A being restricted to long-run states by Say's Law. Yet we preserve in Model B a key property of Model A's Say's Law.

This is the property of Model A's misused Say's Law of providing the basis in the system for a budget constraint of relevance to microeconomics. That is, a budget constraint from which individual quantities of commodities emerge.

However, rather than ridding Model B of this property, we brought it correctly into Model B through the latter system's internal budget constraint.

Individual quantities of commodities emerge from this internal budget constraint which reflects how the system is wholly microeconomic in character.

In contrast, Keynes rid his system of Model A's misused Say's Law by allowing the aggregate demand and supply of commodities in his system to diverge.

Hence Keynes rid his system of the problem of Model A being restricted to long-run states by the system's misused Say's Law. We may now explain in more detail why the microeconomics of the Keynesian system is largely suppressed.

Keynes in ridding his system of Model A's misused Say's Law, rid his system of both properties of Model A's Say's Law that we have described. That is, Keynes rid his system of the property of Model A's misused Say's Law that restricts this system to long-run states.

Moreover, Keynes simultaneously rid his system of the property of Model A's Say's Law of providing the basis in the latter system for a budget constraint of relevance to microeconomics.

Consequently, the Keynesian system in being rid of the property of Model A's misused Say's Law that restricts the latter system to long-run states, is not restricted by the Law to long-run states. However, the microeconomics of the Keynesian system is largely suppressed.

This is because Keynes also rid his system of the property of Model A's misused Say's Law that constitutes a budget constraint of relevance to microeconomics. This accounts for the microeconomics of the Keynesian system being largely suppressed.

In contrast, we rid Model B *only* of the property of Model A's misused Say's Law that restricts the latter system to long-run states.

Hence we did not rid Model B of the property of Model A's misused Say's Law that provides the basis in the system for a budget constraint of relevance to microeconomics.

Instead, we brought this property of Model A's misused Say's Law correctly into Model B through the system's internal budget constraint. Individual quantities of commodities emerge from this internal budget constraint which gives the system a wholly microeconomic character.

In sum, we preserve in Model B the key role of Model A's Say's Law of providing in the latter system the basis for a budget constraint of relevance to microeconomics.

This explains why Model B, unlike the Keynesian system, is wholly microeconomic in character. We may also put this analysis in the following way.

We brought a true identity form of the Law into Model B through expression $W\{f(z) - g(z)\} = 0$. This is the system's internal budget constraint which cannot possibly restrict the system to long-run states.

Moreover, Model B's internal budget constraint reflects how the system is wholly microeconomic in character. This is because individual quantities of commodities demanded and supplied emerge from this internal budget constraint.

Consequently, Model B's internal budget constraint $W\{f(z) - g(z)\} = 0$ has two key roles:

First, it rids Model B of Model A's misused Say's Law by bringing a true identity form of the Law into Model B that cannot possibly restrict the system to long-run states.

Second, Model B's internal budget constraint simultaneously ensures that the system is characterized by a budget constraint out of which individual quantities of commodities demanded (supplied) emerge. This reflects how Model B is wholly microeconomic in character.

9.8 Summary

Keynes held that Model A, the orthodox classical system, is restricted to long-run states by Say's Law. However, we established that while Model A is restricted to long-run states by the Law, this is because of a misused form of Say's Law that characterizes the system.

This misused Say's Law enters Model A because of the inconsistency we uncovered in the system. Hence to resolve the problem of Model A being restricted to long-run states by Say's Law, we needed to rid the system of this inconsistency.

This was accomplished through Model B, this system hence being rid of Model A's misused of Say's Law that restricts the latter system to long-run states. This, moreover, was accomplished in a manner which ensured that Model B is wholly microeconomic in character.

These findings were confirmed in Chapter 6.4 by our bringing a true identity form of the Law into Model B through expression $W\{f(z) - g(z)\} = 0$ which is the system's internal budget constraint. This rid Model B of Model A's misused Say's Law that restricts the latter system to long-run states.

Moreover, expression $W\{f(z) - g(z)\} = 0$ in being a budget constraint, reflects how the system is wholly microeconomic in character. This is because individual quantities of commodities emerge from this internal budget constraint.

Keynes also rid his system of Model A's misused Say's Law that restricts the system to long-run states. This, however, as we have discussed, is accomplished in a manner that accounts for the microeconomics of the Keynesian system being largely suppressed.

This, to review, is on account of Keynes' use of aggregate demand and supply functions to rid his system of Model A's misused Say's Law. However, these functions suppress the microeconomics of the part of the Keynesian system that is based on these functions.

Chapter 10

Issues Concerning Consistency Of Price Systems

10.1 Introduction

There is a basic theme running through this book which is that our revised classical system, Model B, is based wholly on economic principles or economic behavior.

This as discussed in Chapter 8 is in the sense that there is no interference with these principles or behavior in Model B stemming from the non-behavioral Say's Law. On the other hand, the behavior or economic rationale of the orthodox classical system, Model A, is restricted by the non-behavioral Say's Law.

We shall proceed in the chapter by first discussing how we may look on the inconsistency of Model A as causing a gap in the system's behavioral content.

This will assist us in bringing out how Say's Law is misused in Model A. This is because we shall establish that the *non-behavioral Say's Law* is brought into the picture to fill the gap in the system's *behavioral content*.

We shall also review aspects of the controversies that arose in response to Patinkin's claim that Model A is inconsistent in an economic sense.

Next, we have discussed how all price systems are characterized by a general logic this being reflected in the systems being consistent with limitation in resources.

That is, in the quantities of commodities demanded and supplied each summing to the systems' limited resources to hence exhaust these resources. Two conditions are required to bring this logic into a system.

First, we must isolate a variable in the system that reflects the system's limited resources. Second, the commodity demands and supplies determined in the system must each sum to these limited resources.

These are the two conditions that are required to capture a system's general logic; and in this book. we raised the issue of how these two conditions are brought into a system in order to satisfactorily capture the general logic of the system. Then through exploring these issues, we uncovered and resolved the economic inconsistency of Model A, the orthodox classical system.

10.2 Remarks On Model A and Model B

In forming price systems, we need to ensure *from the outset* that the systems reflect behavior that is consistent with limitation in resources.

This was ensured in Model B by our writing the system's demand and supply functions to determine *relative* quantities of commodities demanded (supplied) as functions of the relative prices. These functions from the outset ensure consistency of the system with limited resources.

This is because as the relative prices change, quantities demanded (supplied) adjust in a relative manner to always exhaust the system's limited resources. This reflects how Model B is characterized by an aspect to behavior that ensures consistency of the system with limited resources.

In sum, consistency of Model B with limitation in resources is ensured from the outset in being ensured by the system's new type of functions and hence by the behavior in the system. Let us now consider Model A.

Economists in writing Model A do not ensure *from the outset* that this system reflects consistency with limitation in resources. This is because they do not frame the system's functions so that they ensure consistency of the system with limited resources.

Consequently, there is a gap in the behavioral content of Model A since the system lacks an aspect to behavior aspect that should ensure consistency of the system with limited resources. This accounts for the system being characterized by a surplus equation over the number of unknowns.

Economists then impose Say's Law on the system to eliminate this surplus equation to ensure that the system meets the counting rule; and the Law as we have established in Chapter 5.2, simultaneously ensures that Model A is consistent with limitation in resources.

Hence Say's Law which is non-behavioral in character, comes into the picture to fill the gap in the system's *behavioral content*. This is through the Law ensuring that the system is consistent with limitation in resources.

This, however, accounts for the inconsistency in Model A; since consistency of the system with limitation in resources should be ensured by the behavior in the system rather than by the non-behavioral Say's Law.

10.3 Controversies Concerning Consistency Of Model A and Model B

We discussed in Chapter 7 how Patinkin held that Model A is inconsistent in an economic sense. Moreover, we also discussed how some economists, in contrast, took Model A to be consistent on the basis that it can be solved for equilibrium. That is, on the basis that the system meets the counting rule.

However, this book shows that taking Model A to be consistent solely on the basis of the system meeting the counting rule is an unsatisfactory approach to ensuring consistency of the system.

Archibald and Lipsey were among several economists who held that Model A is consistent in that it can be solved for equilibrium. [16] Yet Archibald and Lipsey also recognized as Patinkin had held, that Model A lacked market equilibrating processes that are needed to determine the system's price level.

Hence Archibald and Lipsey concluded that Patinkin's real-balance approach was indeed useful in bringing market equilibrating processes into the system to move it to equilibrium.

Nonetheless, Archibald and Lipsey's main point was that Model A is consistent in that it can be solved for equilibrium since the system meets the counting rule. In this way, they defended Model A from Patinkin's charge that the system is inconsistent.

Consequently, Archibald and Lipsey left Model A untouched and hence still characterized by the price level indeterminacy and invalid dichotomy that Patinkin held characterize the system.

True, Model A meets the counting rule as Archibald and Lipsey emphasized. However, this is on account of the non-behavioral Say's Law being imposed on the system to eliminate a surplus equation. Moreover, the Law as discussed in Chapter 5.2, ensures consistency of the system with limited resources.

This brought inconsistency into Model A since the system should be made consistent with limited resources by the behavior in the system. This as we have established is the case with

---

[16] G.C Archibald and R.G. Lipsey, "Monetary and Value Theory: A Critique of Lange and Patinkin", *Review of Economic Studies* (1958), pps. 1-22.

Model B, our revised classical system, this system hence being rid of Model A's inconsistency.

Next, as we discussed in Chapter 7, this accounted for us resolving, through Model B, the problems with Model A that were raised by Patinkin.

These are Model A's price level indeterminacy and associated invalid real-monetary dichotomy. Moreover, we established in Chapter 6 that Model B is also rid of a misused Say's Law that restricts Model A to long-run states.

In sum, we have rid Model B, our revised classical system, of the problems with the orthodox classical system, Model A, that were brought out by Keynes and Patinkin.

These problems, to review, are the restriction of Model A by Say's Law to long-run states, a problem brought out by Keynes, and the system's price level indeterminacy and invalid real-monetary dichotomy, problems brought out by Patinkin.

10.4 Inconsistency And Surplus Demand And Supply Functions In Model A.

Model A's demand and supply functions lead to a surplus equation over the number of unknowns; and we showed that this is due to an economic inconsistency in the system.

This inconsistency arose because the system's functions, and hence the behavior in the system, does not ensure that the system is consistent with limitation in resources.

This, in turn, leads to Model A being initially inconsistent which is reflected in there being a surplus equation over the number of unknowns. Hence Model A's functions should be revised so that they ensure consistency of the system with limited resources.

Economists instead commonly impose Say's Law on the system to eliminate Model A's surplus equation to make the system meet the counting rule.

Next, the Law as we established in Chapter 5.2, also ensures that the system is consistent with limitation in resources. This means of ensuring consistency of Model A with limitation in resources, however, brings the inconsistency we have uncovered into the system.

This is because consistency of the system with limitation in resources should be ensured by the system's behavior or economic rationale rather than by the non-behavioral Say's Law.

Model A's inconsistency hence had to be resolved by our transforming Model A's functions into the demand and supply functions of Model B.

These latter functions, which we shall refer to as relative demand and supply functions, and hence the behavior in Model B, ensure consistency of the system with limited resources, Model B hence being rid of Model A's economic inconsistency.

Model B's functions, moreover, as we established in Chapter 6.3, automatically ensure equality of the number of independent equations and the number of unknowns in Model B. As a result, there is no need to eliminate a surplus demand and supply function from Model B. Let us now consider Model A.

Model A, of course, reflects consistency with limitation in resources. However, consistency with limited resources is ensured in the system through a misused Say's Law being imposed on the system to eliminate a surplus equation.

This results in one demand and one supply function being made redundant and hence being eliminated from Model A to ensure that the system meets the counting rule.

However, the initial existence of Model A's surplus functions is a result of the system being inconsistent with limited resources. The system is then made consistent with limited resources but in an incorrect manner.

That is, Say's Law in being used to eliminate a surplus equation from Model A also ensures consistency of the system with limitation in resources. This brings inconsistency into Model A since consistency with limited resources should be ensured by the behavior in the system.

Clearly, the need to eliminate a surplus equation from Model A is forced on Model A by the economic inconsistency of this system. This is readily confirmed.

When we replaced Model A's functions with the relative demand and supply functions of Model B, these latter functions ensure consistency of Model B with limitation in resources.

As well, Model B's functions automatically lead to equality between the number of independent equations and unknowns in the system. Hence there was now no need to eliminate a surplus equation from Model B.

This means that the initial existence of a surplus equation in Model A is a consequence of the system's economic inconsistency. Furthermore, the elimination of this surplus equation from Model A by imposing Say's Law on the system is a reflection of Model A's inconsistency being incorrectly resolved.

This is because this inconsistency should be resolved in the first place by revision of Model A's demand and supply functions to transform them into Model B's relative demand and supply functions. This is the course followed in this book through Model B.

Model B's functions, in ensuring consistency of the system with limited resources, rids the system of Model A's economic inconsistency. Moreover, these functions also ensure that Model B meets the counting rule.

This approach made the whole issue of the existence of a surplus equation in Model A, and hence the need to eliminate this equation, redundant in the case of Model B.

10.5 Remarks On Consistency Of Price Systems

This book has established through Model B that consistency of a price system, as reflected in equality between the number of the system's independent equations and unknowns, should not be imposed on a system.

Instead, equality between independent equations and unknowns should stem from the system's economic rationale and hence from the system's demand and supply functions. This is readily confirmed by referring to Model A and Model B, the orthodox and revised classical systems.

Model A, to review, is initially characterized by a surplus equation over the number of unknowns. Then Say's Law is imposed on the system to eliminate this surplus equation.

This approach, however, as we have established, brings a misused Say's Law into Model A that restricts the system to long-run states. Let us now consider Model B.

Through Model B's new type of functions, we brought an aspect to behavior into the system that ensures consistency of the system with limited resources. Moreover, this new aspect to behavior, as discussed in Chapter 6.3, ensures that Model B meets the counting rule.

This meant that we did not need Say's Law to ensure consistency of Model B by eliminating a surplus equation from the system. Hence Model B is rid of the misused Say's Law of Model A that is imposed on the latter system to eliminate a surplus equation but which restricts the system to long-run states.

Clearly, this analysis has basic implications for the counting rule that is imposed on orthodox systems such as

Model A to eliminate a surplus equation from the systems. This is to ensure equality between the number of independent equations and the number of unknowns in the systems. This equality must hold in all systems.

However, it must be ensured by consistency of the system's behavior or general economic logic as is the case with Model B. True, the number of independent equations and unknowns are also equal in Model A. However, this is ensured by the counting rule being imposed on this system.

This is through Say's Law being used to eliminate a surplus equation. This, however, brings a misused Say's Law into Model A that restricts the system to long-run states. This problem, however, has been resolved through Model B.

This is because as we established in Chapter 6.3, consistency of Model B in the sense of the system meeting the counting rule is ensured by the behavior in the system. Hence we do not need Model A's Say's Law to ensure that Model B meets the counting rule.

This rids Model B of the misused Say's Law that restricts Model A to long-run states. This is through Model A's misused Say's Law being transformed into a correct Say's Law in Model B. This as we confirmed in Chapter 6.4 is a true identity that cannot possibly restrict the system to long-run states.

10.6 Review Of The Implications Of The Book For The Counting Rule

We have discussed how consistency is imposed on Model A through the imposing of the counting rule on the system. This is through a misused Say's Law being imposed on the system to eliminate a surplus equation. However, this misused Say's Law restricts Model A to long-run states.

We need, of course, to ensure that price systems meet the counting rule. However, we need to apply this rule to Model A in a manner that does not result in the system being restricted to long-run states. This was accomplished in the following way.

Say's Law in being imposed on Model A to eliminate a surplus equation ensures that the system meets the counting rule. However, we established in Chapter 5.2 that the Law simultaneously ensures that Model A is consistent with limitation in resources.

This brings inconsistency into the system; since consistency of the system with limitation in resources should be ensured by the behavior in the system.

This meant that if we could find a behavioral means to ensure consistency of Model A with limited resources, we would avoid having to impose Say's Law on the system to hence avoid the system's inconsistency.

Nonetheless, this alternative behavioral approach to ensuring consistency of Model A with limitation in resources would yet have to ensure that the number of independent equations and the number of unknowns are equal as called for by the counting rule.

We have established that this behavioral substitute for imposing the counting rule on Model B is the new aspect to behavior that we brought into the system. This new aspect to behavior ensures consistency of Model B with limited resources to rid the latter system of Model A's inconsistency.

Moreover, as we established in Chapter 6.3, this new aspect to behavior also ensures consistency of Model B in the sense of ensuring equality between the number of independent equations and unknowns in the system.

Hence through this new aspect to behavior that we brought into Model B, we found a behavioral means of ensuring that the system meets the counting rule.

As a result, we do not have to *impose* consistency on Model B by imposing the counting rule on the system through Say's Law as has to be done in the case of Model A. This, to review, is because Model B meets the counting rule on account of the system's behavior or economic rationale.

This difference between the systems accounts for Model A being restricted to long-run states by an incorrect or misused Say's Law. On the other hand, Model B is not restricted by such an incorrect or misused Say's Law to long-run states.

Instead, as discussed in Chapter 6.4, Model B is characterized by a true identity form of Say's Law that cannot possibly restrict the system to long-run states.

10.7 An Improved Criterion For Ensuring Consistency Of Price Systems

We have established that in bringing into Model B an aspect to behavior that ensures consistency of the system with limited resources, we rid the system of Model A's inconsistency.

Moreover, this also accounts for Model B automatically meeting the counting rule in equating the number of independent equations and the number of unknowns in the system. But Model A is not characterized by the new aspect to behavior that we brought into Model B.

This accounts for there being a surplus equation over the number of unknowns in the system. Say's Law is then imposed on Model A to eliminate this surplus equation to ensure consistency of the system.

However, Model A while seemingly being consistent in meeting the counting rule, is not wholly behavioral in character. This is because as we have discussed, the non-behavioral Say's Law is brought into Model A to fill a gap in the system's behavioral content.

This gap, to review, is due to the aspect to behavior that should ensure consistency of the system with limited resources being missing from the system. This analysis as we shall now discuss, provides the basis for an improved criterion for consistency of a price system.

This new criterion is that for a system to be consistent it must be wholly behavioral in character. This in the present context means that the behavioral content of the system must be wholly free of the non-behavioral Say's Law.

Clearly, Model B meets this criterion since the system as we have established, is wholly behavioral in character. This is reflected, for example, in the Law not being needed to fill a gap in the system's behavioral content.

However, Model A does not meet our new criterion for consistency of a price system since the system is not wholly behavioral in character.

This is because the non-behavioral Say's Law is needed to fill the gap we described that exists in the system's behavioral content. Let us go further into this analysis.

We have discussed how our new criterion for a system to be consistent is that it must be wholly behavioral in character. This is in the sense that the behavioral content of the system must be wholly free of any influence of the non-behavioral Say's Law; and we have established that Model B meets this criterion.

However, price systems to be consistent must also meet the counting rule. That is, the number of independent equations and unknowns must be equal; and this is also the case with Model B.

This is because as we established in Chapter 6.3, the new aspect to behavior that we bring into Model B also ensures that the system meets the counting rule. That is, it ensures that the number of independent equations and unknowns in the system are equal.

In sum, it is not sufficient to ensure consistency of a system simply by establishing that the system meets the counting rule. This is confirmed by Model A since this system, while meeting the counting rule, is yet characterized by the economic inconsistency we have uncovered in the system.

Consequently, to ensure consistency of a system we must ensure that the system is consistent in an economic sense. This will then ensure that the system meets the counting rule. This is confirmed by Model B which in being rid of the economic inconsistency of Model A, automatically meets the counting rule.

10.8 Summary

There is a basic theme running through this book which is that our revised classical system, Model B, is based wholly on economic principles or economic behavior.

This is in the sense that there is no interference with these principles or behavior in Model B stemming from the non-behavioral Say's Law.

On the other hand, the behavior or economic rationale of the orthodox classical system, Model A, is restricted by the non-behavioral Say's Law. This is on account of a misused Say's Law restricting the system to long-run states.

We proceeded by first discussing how we may look on the inconsistency of Model A as causing a gap in the system's behavioral content. This gap arises because the system lacks an aspect to behavior that should ensure consistency of the system with limited resources.

This assisted us in bringing out how Say's Law is misused in Model A. This is because the *non-behavioral* Say's Law is brought into the picture to fill the gap in the system's *behavioral content.*

This is by the Law ensuring consistency of the system with limited resources. Whereas consistency of the system with limited resources should be ensured by the behavior in the system as is the case with Model B.

We also reviewed aspects of the controversies that arose in response to Patinkin's claim that Model A is inconsistent in an economic sense. Finally, in Section 10.7, we discussed how our analysis allows us to arrive at an improved criterion for ensuring consistency of price systems.

Chapter 11

Integrating Microeconomic And Macroeconomic Systems

11.1 Introduction

We have rid Model B, our revised classical system, of an inconsistency in the orthodox classical system, Model A; and we shall discuss in this chapter how Model B, together with the Keynesian system, provides the basis to form a system to be denoted as Model C in which microeconomic and macroeconomic analysis are complementary and are hence integrated in the system.

11.2 Integrating Microeconomic And Macroeconomic Systems

Model B, our revised classical system, reflects behavior that is consistent with limitation in resources, the system hence reflecting what we referred to as the general *economic* logic of price systems.

We took the limited resources of our systems to be reflected in the systems' overall flow of output or income. Referring to Model A, we saw that we imposed on this system an overall output or income variable W that we derived from Say's Law. Hence this variable is also taken to reflect the system's limited flow of resources.

Model B, however, lacks an overall output or income variable since the system's functions determine only relative quantities of commodities. Hence an overall output or income variable had to be brought into the system from the outside.

We proceeded to impose on Model B the same variable W that is imbedded in Model A. However, there is a significant difference between the systems. This is because we purposefully impose W on Model B whereas W is necessarily imbedded in

Model A. This is because it stems from Say's Law that is imposed on Model A to ensure consistency of the system.

Next, just as we could purposefully impose W on Model B, we may also impose a substitute for this variable that also reflects the system's overall output or income or the system's limited flow of resources.

We shall proceed to do so by setting out a system, Model C, which will be based on the same behavioral rationale that underlies Model B. Hence Model C, like Model B, will reflect behavior that is consistent with limitation in resources.

However, we shall now take the overall output or income of the *Keynesian system* rather than the W of Model B, to reflect Model C's limited flow of resources.

We shall now establish that Model C is rid of Model A's inconsistency in a manner that integrates microeconomic analysis and Keynesian macroeconomic analysis.

This integration is possible because Model C, in being based on the microeconomic approach of Model B, reflects behavior that is consistent with limitation in resources. *However, these resources in Model C now stem from the Keynesian system.*

Next, since Model C like Model B reflects behavior that is consistent with limitation in resources, Model C is rid of the inconsistency we have uncovered in Model A.

However, this is accomplished through Model C in a manner that reflects how microeconomic analysis and Keynesian macroeconomic analysis in the system are *complementary* and are hence integrated in the system.

This is because we require both the microeconomics of Model C that stems from Model B *and* Keynesian macroeconomic analysis, to ensure that Model C is rid of the inconsistency of Model A.

Hence through Model C, we integrate microeconomic and macroeconomic analysis by finding *complementary* roles in this system for these analyses. This is reflected in Model C's microeconomics through functions $f(z)$ and $g(z)$ dealing with behavior that is *consistent* with limitation in resources.

While Model C's macroeconomics deals with behavior that *determines* these resources. This is through Keynesian macroeconomic analysis determining an overall output or income variable that reflects Model C's limited flow of resources.

In sum, on account of the inconsistency of Model A, an overall output or income variable is imbedded in the system on account of Say's Law.

However, since Model B is rid of Model A's inconsistency and hence of Say's Law, we find that we have the ability to choose to impose W on Model B. This is because this variable is not necessarily imbedded in   Model B as is the case with Model A.

By the same token, we could also choose to replace W in Model B with a variable that reflects the overall output or income of the Keynesian system.

This leads to Model C in which microeconomic and macroeconomic analysis are complementary and are hence integrated in the system. Let us go further into these analyses.

11.3 Contrasting Model B And Model C

We first show Model B, our revised classical system below:

Model B

11. $\quad D_j \equiv F_j'\left[W, f(z)\right]$

12. $\quad S_j \equiv G_j'\left[W, g(z)\right]$

13. $\quad E_j'[W\{f(z) - g(z)\} = 0] = 0$

This system, to review, on account of functions $f(z)$ and $g(z)$, reflects behavior that ensures consistency of the system with limitation in resources.

Now since Model B deals with relative quantities of commodities, the system cannot possibly determine a variable that reflects the system's overall output or income which we take to reflect the system's limited flow of resources.

However, since we had to have such a variable in Model B that reflects the system's limited resources, such a variable had to be brought into the system from outside the system.

Moreover, we derived a variable that we denoted by W from Say's Law, see Chapter 5.2. This variable as we have discussed, reflects Model B's long-run overall output or income which represents the system's limited flow of resources.

In sum, the variable W that appears in Model B's demand and supply functions is brought into the system from outside the system, namely, from Say's Law.

This need to bring the variable W from the outside into Model B opened up an avenue to integrating microeconomic and macroeconomic analysis through Model C.

This is because we could also bring a substitute for W from the outside, that is a W that reflects the overall output or income of the Keynesian system. Model C appears below:

Model C

14. $\quad D_j \equiv F_j'\left[W', f(z)\right]$

15. $\quad S_j \equiv G_j'\left[W', g(z)\right]$

16. $\quad E_j'\left[W'\{f(z) - g(z)\} = 0\right] = 0$

Model C reflects the same behavioral approach that characterizes Model B. Hence Model C, like Model B, reflects behavior that is consistent with limitation in resources.

However, we took the overall output or income of the *Keynesian system,* which we denote by W', to reflect Model C's limited flow of resources.

Model C, in reflecting the same behavioral rationale as Model B, reflects behavior that is consistent with limitation in resources.

This is ensured in a manner through Model C that reflects how microeconomic and macroeconomic analysis in the system are complementary and are hence integrated in the system.

This complementarity arises because the microeconomic functions $f(z)$ and $g(z)$ of Model C operate on W' to determine relative quantities of commodities demanded and supplied.

These each adjust in a relative manner to exhaust the system's limited flow of resources W' to ensure consistency of the system with limited resources. *However, these resources in Model C stem from the macroeconomic Keynesian system.*

This is a reflection of how microeconomic and macroeconomic analysis in Model C are complementary and are hence integrated in the system. Let us go further into why we could integrate microeconomic and macroeconomic systems.

Let us for the present analysis define a complete system as one that determines relative prices and also has a W variable, that is, a variable that reflects the system's overall output or income.

Now Model A determines relative prices and also has a W variable. However, this latter variable stems from Say's Law that is required to ensure consistency of the system.

That is, Model A in determining relative prices necessarily becomes a complete system. This as we have discussed, means that the system cannot possibly be integrated with the Keynesian system.

Whereas Model B is such that it determines relative prices while being an incomplete system in lacking an overall output or income variable.

This allowed us to bring an overall output or income variable from the Keynesian system, namely W' into Model B. This led to Model C in which microeconomic and macroeconomic analysis are complementary and are hence integrated in the system.

11.4 Remarks On Integrating Microeconomic And Macroeconomic Systems

Clearly, we could only integrate microeconomic and macroeconomic systems through Model C by first resolving the inconsistency we uncover in the orthodox classical system Model A.

This allowed us to arrive at Model B, our revised classical system. Model B then formed the basis for Model C into which we could integrate microeconomic and macroeconomic analysis.

We shall now review why Model A, the orthodox classical system, unlike Model B, cannot possibly provide the basis to integrate microeconomic and macroeconomic analysis.

Model A is characterized by a surplus equation with Say's Law then usually being imposed on the system to eliminate this equation.

Next, as discussed in Chapter 5.2, we took the variable W from Say's Law, this variable reflecting Model A's overall output or income. *This means that Model A masks the true nature of the classical system as being an incomplete system like Model B.*

This is because Say's Law brings an overall output or income variable into Model A, this system hence seemingly being complete in being characterized by an overall output or income variable.

Consequently, the process whereby we could bring a Keynesian overall output or income variable into Model C is wholly suppressed in Model A. Let us review how we resolved this problem of Model A through Model B.

We have seen that while Model B is rid of the inconsistency of Model A, Model B is a system that cannot possibly determine an overall output or income variable. This brought out how Model B is an incomplete system in the sense of lacking such an overall output or income variable.

Next, we formed Model C using the same microeconomic rationale that characterizes Model B. Hence Model C like Model B is incomplete in lacking an overall output or income variable.

However, this incompleteness of Model C then allowed us to bring a Keynesian overall output or income variable into the system. This as we established, accounted for microeconomic and macroeconomic analysis in Model C being complementary and hence integrated in the system.

Clearly, also, Model C is not restricted to long-run states but can move into alternative states. This is because Model C is characterized by a Keynesian overall output of income variable, namely, W'.

This variable changes as the Keynesian system moves to alternative states to cause the overall Model C to move to similar states. Yet microeconomic and macroeconomic analysis remain integrated in whatever state the system may describe.

This is on account of microeconomic functions such as $f(z)$ and $g(z)$ always ensuring consistency of the system with limitation in resources. However, these resources in Model C, which we denoted by W', stem from the Keynesian system.

11.5 Review Of The Systems Set Out In The Book

Model A', the preliminary form of Model A that was set out in Chapter 3.3 appears below:

Model A'

1. $D_j \equiv F(p_j)$
2. $S_j \equiv G(p_j)$
3. $E(p_j) = 0$

We then imposed the "homogeneity postulate" on Model A' to form Model A below, this system representing the orthodox classical system.

Behavior in Model A is rational in the sense that quantities demanded (supplied) depend on the real or relative prices, the z, as opposed to the money prices:

Model A

4. $D_j \equiv F_j[z]$

5. $S_j \equiv G_j[z]$

6. $E_j[z] = 0$

Next, we formed Model B below, our revised classical system. We then established in detail that Model B is rid of the inconsistency we uncovered in Model A.

This as discussed in Chapter 6 then accounted for Model B being rid of a misused Say's Law that restricts Model A to long-run states.

As well, we established in Chapter 7 that Model B is rid of the price level price level indeterminacy and invalid real-monetary dichotomy, of the neoclassical form of Model A.

Model B

11. $D_j \equiv F_j'\big[W, f(z)\big]$

12. $S_j \equiv G_j'\big[W, g(z)\big]$

13. $E_j'[W\{f(z) - g(z)\} = 0] = 0$

Finally, in the present chapter, we formed Model C below:

Model C

14. $D_j \equiv F_j'\big[W', f(z)\big]$

15. $S_j \equiv G_j'\big[W', g(z)\big]$

16. $E_j'\big[W'\{f(z) - g(z)\} = 0\big] = 0$

Model C as we have discussed in detail, is a system in which microeconomic analysis and macroeconomic analysis are complementary and are hence integrated in the system.

11.6   Summary

This book has established that the orthodox classical system, Model A, is subject to an economic inconsistency. This inconsistency arises because the system lacks an aspect to behavior that should ensure consistency of the system with limited resources.

This inconsistency as we established in detail, accounts for the system being restricted by Say's Law to long-run states. Hence the system is dichotomized from the Keynesian short-run or macroeconomic system.

However, we formed a revised classical system, Model B, that is rid of Model A's inconsistency. We then formed Model C that is based on the same general rationale as Model B.

We then established in detail that microeconomic analysis and Keynesian macroeconomic analysis in Model C are complementary and are hence are integrated in the system.

To review, Model C's microeconomic functions, in reflecting the same rationale as those of Model B, account for Model C reflecting behavior that is consistent with limitation in resources. Next, the limited resources of our systems are reflected in the systems' overall output or income.

Model C, however, like Model B deals only with relative quantities of commodities hence Model C, also like Model B, cannot possibly determine an overall output or income variable. Hence such a variable, as was also the case with Model B, had to be brought into the system from the outside.

Next, we took Model C's limited flow of resources to be reflected in the overall output or income of the Keynesian system. Hence Model C in being based on the microeconomic approach of Model B, reflects behavior that is consistent with limitation in resources. The system hence being rid of the inconsistency of Model A.

However, this is accomplished through Model C in a manner that integrates microeconomic analysis and Keynesian macroeconomic analysis.

This is because we require Model C's microeconomic analysis that stems from Model B, to ensure consistency of the system with limited resources. However, these resources in Model C stem from the Keynesian macroeconomic system. Hence microeconomic and macroeconomic analysis in Model C are complementary which integrates these analyses.

Chapter 12

Summarizing The Book

Economists form price systems by writing demand and supply functions of particular systems then ensuring consistency of the systems. This approach, however, leads to systems that are restricted in generality.

This is reflected, for example, in orthodox microeconomic and macroeconomic systems being dichotomized which subjects the systems to additional problems.

Orthodox microeconomic and macroeconomic systems are dichotomized because neither system reflects what we referred to as the *general economic logic* of price systems. This is a logic that applies to all price systems irrespective of the different forms of behavior of individual systems.

We suggest in this book that prior to writing specific price systems, we should first isolate this general economic logic of price systems. We should then write systems that reflect different forms of behavior, to conform to this general economic logic.

This is the approach to price systems set out in this book, an approach that rid orthodox price systems of the dichotomy between microeconomic and macroeconomic systems and of basic problems that arise on account of this dichotomy.

However, to bring the general economic logic to which we referred into orthodox price systems required resolving an inconsistency in the systems. Let us describe this inconsistency.

Price systems are all necessarily *subject* to limitation in resources. Hence the systems should reflect *consistency* with limitation in resources.

We defined consistency with limited resources to be reflected in the quantities of commodities demanded and supplied in price systems each summing to the systems' limited resources to hence exhaust these resources.

Clearly, consistency with limitation in resources applies across all price systems. Hence we may look on consistency with limited resources as reflecting the *general logic* of the systems. That is, a logic that characterizes all price systems irrespective of the differing forms of behavior of individual systems.

Next, we took the orthodox classical system which we referred to as Model A, as representative of orthodox microeconomic price systems. As well, we set out a revised classical system, Model B, which we took as representative of our new microeconomic systems.

We then established that the behavior in Model A, the orthodox classical system, does not ensure that the system is consistent with limitation in resources.

This is because an aspect to the behavior of individuals and firms that should ensure consistency of the system with limited resources is missing from the system.

Next, since all price systems must reflect consistency with limitation in resources, consistency with limitation in resources is ensured in resources in Model A in a non-behavioral manner.

This as we established in Chapter 5.2 is by Say's Law rather than by the behavior in the system. This accounted for the inconsistency we uncovered in Model A.

This is because consistency of a system with limitation in resources should be ensured by the behavior in the system and hence by the system's demand and supply functions.

Model A does reflect the *general logic* of price systems in reflecting consistency with limitation in resources. However, Model A does not reflect the *general economic logic* of price systems. This is because consistency of the system with limitation in resources is not ensured by the behavior in the system.

Instead, consistency with limitation in resources, as we discussed in Chapter 5.2 is ensured in Model A in a non-behavioral manner in being ensured by Say's Law. Let us now consider Model B, our revised form of Model A.

Consistency with limitation in resources is ensured in Model B by the system's behavior or economic rationale. This is because the system's demand and supply functions determine *relative* quantities of commodities demanded (supplied) as functions of the relative prices.

Hence as the relative prices change, quantities of commodities demanded (supplied) adjust in a relative manner to exhaust the system's limited resources. This means that the behavior in Model B, rather than Say's Law, ensures consistency of the system with limited resources.

Consequently, Model B is rid of the inconsistency of Model A, an inconsistency which, to review, arises because consistency of the latter system with limited resources is not ensured by the behavior in the system but is ensured by the non-behavioral Say's Law.

In sum, Model B in being rid of the inconsistency of Model A, reflects the *general economic logic* that should characterize all price systems. This is because consistency of the system with limited resources is ensured by the behavior in the system.

Whereas Model A does not reflect this general *economic logic* since as discussed, consistency of the system with limited resources is not ensured by the behavior in the system but is ensured by the non-behavioral Say's Law.

We then established that Model B is rid of a key problem with Model A that was brought out by Keynes. Keynes has held that Model A, which we use to represent the orthodox classical system, is restricted by Say's Law to long-run states.

However, we established that this is on account of a misused Say's Law that characterizes the system. Hence the solution to this problem is to replace Model A's misused Say's Law with a correct form of the Law. This was the approach to Say's Law followed in this book.

We proceeded by first establishing that Model A's misused Say's Law is an external budget constraint. This is not a true identity and it restricts the system to long-run states.

However, in ridding Model B of Model A's inconsistency, we transformed Model A's external budget constraint into an internal budget constraint in Model B. This latter budget constraint in being internal to Model B, cannot possibly restrict the system to long-run states.

This as discussed in Chapter 6.4, gives Model B's internal budget constraint the property of being a true identity form of Say's Law. Hence it cannot possibly restrict the system to long-run states.

In sum, Model B, our revised classical system, is not restricted by Say's Law to long-run states. Moreover, as discussed in Chapter 7, Model B is also rid of the price level indeterminacy and invalid real-monetary of the neoclassical form of Model A, problems that were brought out by Patinkin.

There are also key implications of the book for what we referred to as the "counting rule." This rule is imposed on orthodox systems such as Model A to eliminate a surplus equation from the system.

This is in order to equate the number of independent equations and the number of unknowns to ensure consistency of the system. However, this rule is imposed on Model A by Say's Law which as we noted, is used to eliminate a surplus equation from the system. However, the Law restricts the system to long-run states.

In contrast, the behavior in Model B, as we established in Chapter 6.3, ensures that the system meets the counting rule. These findings allowed us to arrive in Chapter 10.7 at an improved criterion for ensuring consistency of price systems.

This new criterion is that for a system to be consistent it must be wholly behavioral in character. Clearly, Model B meets this condition in being rid of Model A's misused Say's Law.

However, price systems to be consistent must also meet the counting rule. That is, the number of independent equations and unknowns must be equal; and this is also the case with Model B.

This is because as we established in Chapter 6.3, the behavior or economic rationale of Model B ensures that the system meets the counting in ensuring that the number of independent equations and unknowns in the system are equal.

Now economists usually take Model A to be consistent on the grounds that it meets the counting rule. Clearly, however, this is not a satisfactory approach to ensuring consistency of the system.

This is because hidden within the system is the economic inconsistency that we have uncovered. True, price systems must meet the counting rule to be consistent. However, as we established through Model B, this must be ensured by the system's behavior or economic rational.

Moreover, this can only be ensured by the system being consistent in an economic sense; and we ensured that Model B is consistent in an economic sense by our ridding the system of the inconsistency we have uncovered in Model A.

Our analysis also led to a further system, Model C, a system in which microeconomic and macroeconomic analysis are complementary and are hence integrated in the system.

To review, Model B, our revised classical system, reflects behavior that is consistent with limitation in resources. However, Model B deals with relative quantities of commodities.

Hence the system cannot possibly determine a variable that reflects the system's overall output or income. Consequently, such a variable had to be brought into the system from the outside.

Now Model B is a long-run system; and in forming the system we used a variable W that we derived from Say's Law in Chapter 5.2. This variable reflects the system's long-run overall output or income, this overall output or income also being taken to reflect the system's limited flow of resources.

Next, in Chapter 11 we formed a new system, Model C. This is a system that is based on the same microeconomic approach as that of Model B. Hence Model C, like Model B, reflects behavior that is consistent with limitation in resources.

Moreover, Model C like Model B cannot possibly determine an overall output or income variable that we may take to reflect the system's limited flow of resources.

However, we took the overall output or income of the *Keynesian system* to reflect Model C's limited flow of resources. This meant that we rid Model C of Model A's inconsistency in a manner that integrates microeconomic analysis and Keynesian macroeconomic analysis.

This integration was possible because Model C, in being based on the approach of Model B, reflects behavior that is consistent with limitation in resources. *However, these resources in Model C stem from the Keynesian system.*

Next, since Model C reflects behavior that is consistent with limitation in resources, the system is rid of the inconsistency we have uncovered in Model A.

However, this is accomplished through Model C in a manner that reflects how microeconomic analysis and Keynesian macroeconomic analysis in the system are *complementary* and are hence integrated in the system.

This, to review, is because we require both the microeconomic approach of Model C, that stems from Model B, and Keynesian macroeconomic analysis, to ensure that Model C is rid of the inconsistency of Model A. That is, to ensure that Model C reflects behavior that is consistent with limitation in resources.

Clearly also, Model C can move to alternative states since there is a variable in the system that reflects the overall output or income of the Keynesian system.

Hence this variable changes as the Keynesian system moves to alternative states which causes the overall Model C to move to similar states. This reflects how Model C has a macroeconomic character.

Yet the system is also microeconomic in character in whatever state it may describe. This, as we have illustrated in detail, is on account of the microeconomic analysis that characterizes Model C.

This microeconomic analysis which stems from Model B, ensures consistency of Model C with limited resources in whatever state the system may describe, these resources, to review, reflecting the overall output or income of the Keynesian system.

Let us now review why Model A, unlike Model B, cannot possibly provide the basis to integrate microeconomic and macroeconomic analysis.

We have discussed how we need to impose Say's Law on Model A to eliminate a surplus equation to ensure consistency of the system.

Next, the Law as we established in Chapter 5.2, brings an overall output or income variable into the system. Consequently, Model A masks the true nature of the classical system as an incomplete system.

This is because Say's Law brings an overall output or income variable into the system. Model A is hence seemingly complete in the sense of being characterized by an overall output or income variable.

Hence the whole process whereby we could bring a Keynesian overall output or income variable into Model C is suppressed in Model A. Let us review how we resolved this problem of Model A through Model B.

Through ridding Model B of the inconsistency of Model A, we rid Model B of Say's Law. This brought out how Model B is an incomplete system in the sense of lacking an overall output or income variable.

This is because since Model B is rid of the Law, the system is also rid of the overall output or income variable W that we derived from the Law. This reflects how Model B is incomplete in lacking an overall output or income variable.

Next, we used the microeconomic approach of Model B to form Model C, this latter system hence being an incomplete system like Model B in lacking an overall output or income variable.

This very incompleteness of Model C then allowed us to incorporate a Keynesian overall output or income variable into the system.

This as we have discussed in detail, led to microeconomic and macroeconomic analysis being complementary in Model C, these analyses hence being integrated in the system. Let us review why we could integrate microeconomic and macroeconomic systems.

We defined a complete system as one that determines relative prices and also has a W variable. That is, a variable that reflects the system's overall output or income.

Now Model A determines relative prices and also has a W variable. However, this latter variable stems from Say's Law that is required to ensure consistency of the system.

That is, Model A necessarily becomes a complete system. This as we have discussed, means that the system cannot possibly be integrated with the Keynesian system.

Whereas Model B is such that it determines relative prices while being an incomplete system in lacking an overall output or income variable.

This allowed us to bring such a variable from the Keynesian system into Model B. This led to Model C in which microeconomic and macroeconomic analysis are complementary and are hence integrated in the system.

Now it is no accident that in capturing the general *economic* logic of price systems, we integrate microeconomic and macroeconomic price systems.

Price systems should have both a microeconomic and a macroeconomic aspect. Hence the systems' general economic logic should reflect how the systems have this dual microeconomic-macroeconomic character.

However, orthodox price systems are dichotomized into microeconomic and macroeconomic systems. This means that the general economic logic of price systems is dispersed between these orthodox microeconomic and macroeconomic systems.

Consequently, in correctly capturing the general economic logic of price systems, we are able to form systems in which microeconomic and macroeconomic analysis are integrated.

That is, our analysis ensures that the general economic logic of price systems is not dispersed between microeconomic and macroeconomic systems as in orthodox analysis.

However, to ensure this required resolving an inconsistency in orthodox microeconomic price systems such as Model A, an inconsistency we have covered in detail.

Now the orthodox classical system which we represent by Model A predated Keynesian analysis. However, when Keynes set out his macroeconomic system, this latter system remained dichotomized from the orthodox classical system.

Next, we found that Model A lacks an aspect to the behavior of individuals and firms that ensures consistency of the system with limited resources. However, we brought this aspect to behavior into Model B, our revised classical system.

We then drew on Model B and the Keynesian system to form Model C in which microeconomic and macroeconomic analysis are integrated.

107

Thus the microeconomics of Model C that stems from functions such as $f(z)$ and $g(z)$ of Model B, ensures consistency of Model C with limited resources.

While these resources stem from the Keynesian macroeconomic system. Hence microeconomic and macroeconomic analysis in Model C are complementary which integrates these analyses.

Clearly, the overall rationale of the book stems from our writing relative quantities of commodities in Model B to depend on the relative prices. This accounted for Model B being rid of the inconsistency of Model A and of basic problems that characterize the latter system.

These problems include the restriction of Model A by Say's Law to long-run states and the price level indeterminacy and invalid real-monetary dichotomy of the neoclassical form of Model A.

Next, the writing of Model A to make quantities of commodities depend on the relative prices imbedded an overall output or income variable into the system. This explained why we could not possibly integrate Model A and the Keynesian system.

However, we removed this overall output or income variable from Model B by writing relative quantities rather than quantities in this system to depend on the relative prices. Model B as we established in detail could then be integrated with the Keynesian system to form Model C.

Finally, many aspects of our systems were suppressed or omitted in order to assist us in focusing on the main theme of the book. Namely, isolating the general economic logic of price systems. However, the writer in unpublished work is covering many of these aspects of our systems that were omitted.

Thus the systems in the book are being based precisely on the maximization behavior of the individual and the firm. Next, while the focus of much of our analysis was on long-run systems, we need to form short-run forms of the systems.

Moreover, we need to take into account the effects on our systems of the distribution of incomes and resources among individuals and firms.

Index

Printed in the United States
by Baker & Taylor Publisher Services